"This book is a crucial resource for pastors, church leaders, counselors, and caring helpers to navigate the often confusing and murky waters of domestic abuse. We must stop making the same mistakes. Lives are lost, women are harmed, and children are impacted. We must do better. This book will show you how."

Leslie Vernick, Counselor; coach; speaker; author of *The Emotionally Destructive Relationship* and *The Emotionally Destructive Marriage*

"Reading this book is like sitting in on a Q&A session with some of the most skilled and informed biblical counselors specializing in the topic of abuse—except that the authors have not only supplied you with the answers but with the questions as well. Anyone who has ever wondered about how to help people affected by abuse but didn't know where to start will find concrete and comprehensive guidance here."

David and Krista Dunham, Sparrow and Heart Soul Care; authors of *Table for Two: Biblical Counsel for Eating Disorders*

"Like murky water, domestic abuse has a lot of suspended sediment that's hard to see through as you're trying to rescue people. What rescuers need is a way to see clearly and a plan to help. This book provides both—a biblical framework and a practical strategy for helping hurting families."

Jeremy Pierre, Dean, The Billy Graham School of Missions, Evangelism, and Ministry and Lawrence & Charlotte Hoover Professor of Biblical Counseling, The Southern Baptist Theological Seminary; author of *The Dynamic Heart in Daily Life*; coauthor of *When Home Hurts*

"Chris Moles has assembled a team of people who are competent in their field, biblically faithful, and write with clarity and conviction. There's no abstracted theology here, but solid counsel from Scripture about how to navigate the complex world of abuse and serve the families it entangles. Read, pray, grieve the evil that is abuse, and move humbly to help those most in need."

Jonathan D. Holmes, Executive Director, Fieldstone Counseling

"This book is a practical resource for pastors, counselors, and individuals dedicated to fostering healing, restoration, and safety in the lives of those affected by domestic abuse. It gives insightful guidance on essential topics to help you respond with compassion, grace, and biblical wisdom. This book is a must-have for any helper!"

Eliza Huie, Director of Counseling, McLean Bible Church; licensed clinical and biblical counselor

"I'm both brokenhearted and overjoyed to offer this endorsement. I'm brokenhearted because the blight of domestic abuse is as shockingly prevalent in the church as in the culture. I'm overjoyed because the writers of this practical manual represent some of the best counsel the church has to offer. Sadly, this book is desperately needed. Happily, it's finally here now for you. Buy it. Buy copies for your church leaders. Let's change the narrative to be one of joyful understanding and solid support."

Elyse Fitzpatrick, Author

Caring for Families Caught in Domestic Abuse

Caring for Families Caught in Domestic Abuse

A Guide toward Protection, Refuge, and Hope

Chris Moles, Editor

New Growth Press, Greensboro, NC 27401
newgrowthpress.com

Cover Design: Studio Gearbox, studiogearbox.com
Interior Typesetting and e-book: Lisa Parnell, lparnellbookservices.com

ISBN: 978-1-64507-258-4 (Print)
ISBN: 978-1-64507-259-1 (E-book)

Library of Congress Cataloging-in-Publication Data on file

Printed in the United States of America

30 29 28 27 26 25 24 23 1 2 3 4 5

This book is a labor of love to those we serve.

We dedicate this book to those caught
in the destructive power of domestic abuse,
to Christ's church and to our families who help us serve.

....

Contents

INTRODUCTION

....

Preparing for the Complexity

Chris Moles

Occasionally I have been introduced as someone who deals with a very controversial topic. Each time this has happened, I have been struck by that statement and thought to myself or even said aloud, "What is controversial about wanting to protect women and children?" Although protecting women and children should not be controversial for Christians, it must be admitted that domestic abuse is a complex problem, and addressing those complexities in the context of the larger church community presents challenges. Domestic abuse situations reveal our theology and practice, and we may disagree with one another on how to best handle them. These disagreements can lead to a climate of conflict or even controversy.

As you read the chapters of this book, you may even notice differences in how each author addresses domestic abuse. This is largely due to differences in our backgrounds and the populations we most often work with. For instance, Darby Strickland, Joy Forrest, and Kïrsten Christianson have spent far more time working directly with victims of domestic abuse through counseling and advocacy. Greg Wilson and Beth Broom have worked as licensed therapists with a variety of complex counseling issues, and Greg has also worked closely with perpetrators through counseling and in faith-based Men of Peace (MOP) groups. I have spent the last seventeen years working primarily with perpetrators in both individual biblical counseling and through court-ordered educational groups, as well as through Men of Peace. Of course, all of our contributors have dedicated a great deal of time and energy to educating and serving the church in this important work. Part of our goal in bringing together this group of authors was to offer our readers a more nuanced and complete picture of domestic abuse and a wider array of best practices for responding to it than any one of us could have offered on our own.

My hope is that this book will help pastors, elders, deacons, counselors, and other church leaders move toward greater unity in how they respond to domestic abuse, and thereby prevent or lessen some of the potential conflicts and missteps. Will this book assuage all the discomfort one may have with an approach, or fully answer all the questions and concerns that could arise in cases of domestic abuse? Of course not, but it can provide you with some shared language and information, create an opportunity for deeper dialogue within your context, and help you identify where further education is needed to more effectively care for victims and confront abusers. Before you turn to the chapters that deal with specific aspects of domestic abuse care, I'd like to take the remaining pages of this introduction to address some of the most common questions people have about domestic abuse.

What Is Domestic Abuse?

To effectively minister to families caught in domestic abuse, we must begin by having a shared understanding of what domestic abuse entails. It involves a pattern of behaviors used by one partner to maintain power and control over another partner in an intimate relationship. These behaviors may include physical, sexual, emotional, or financial abuse, and they can have severe and long-lasting effects on the victim's mental and physical health, as well as their overall quality of life. How may your care team define domestic abuse? Developing a shared understanding of what is (and is not) domestic abuse will lay the foundation for a wise response.

Why Must the Church Address Domestic Abuse?

Domestic abuse is a pervasive issue that affects individuals across all demographics, including religious communities. According to the National Coalition Against Domestic Violence (NCADV), approximately one in three women and one in four men have experienced some form of physical violence by an intimate partner within their lifetime.[1] Researchers suggest that domestic abuse occurs within Christian communities at a similar rate as in secular communities.[2] Therefore, the church cannot leave the issue solely to secular agencies such as psychologists, police officers, or courts, but rather must look for ways to partner with existing agencies, as well as fulfill our unique calling to provide hope and redemption through the gospel.

There are several reasons why the church must be involved in responding to domestic abuse. First, if abuse is happening within the church body, it is undoubtedly a church problem that requires our response. Additionally, the church may be the only organization that is aware of the abuse or the only place that the abused will go to for help or the abuser will listen to for rebuke. Domestic abuse also damages our Christian witness since the relationship between husband and wife is intended to be a picture of the relationship between Christ and the church. God cares for the oppressed, and we are called to be like Christ, who came to proclaim freedom for the captives and release for the oppressed. The church must actively engage in addressing domestic abuse, whether by offering resources, counseling, or support groups.

---

1. National Coalition Against Domestic Violence, domestic violence statistics, https://ncadv.org/statistics.

2. Nancy Nason-Clark, "The Prevalence of Abuse and Violence in the Christian Home," *Journal of Family Violence* 19, no. 2 (2004): 115–25; David M. Barnes, and Ilan H. Meyer, "Religious Affiliation, Internalized Homophobia, and Mental Health in Lesbians, Gay Men, and Bisexuals," *American Journal of Orthopsychiatry* 82, no. 4 (2012): 505–15.

Who Commits Domestic Abuse?

Spend some time with anyone who focuses on the issue of domestic abuse, and you will quickly realize that they generally refer to men as abusers and women as victims or survivors. This can be confusing to some people because it seems to imply that we think only men can be abusive. Is it not true that women can perpetrate these acts as well? If we're directly asked, we would all affirm that of course women can perpetrate acts of violence and abuse. It's important to note that women who commit acts of abuse are more likely to harm children rather than their intimate partners. According to the National Child Abuse and Neglect Data System, in the United States, mothers were involved in 40.3 percent of child abuse and neglect cases, while fathers were involved in 36.9 percent of cases.[3] On the other hand, most male victims of abuse experienced childhood abuse rather than intimate partner violence. A study by the Centers for Disease Control and Prevention found that one in six men (16.2 percent) experienced sexual abuse before the age of eighteen, and one in four men (24.8 percent) experienced physical violence by a parent or caregiver during childhood.[4] This illustrates the need to address abuse and violence across the lifespan, including providing support and resources for male victims of childhood abuse.

No one is denying that women represent a significant number of child abusers, men represent a significant number of childhood abuse victims, and each of the contributors to this book has seen some female abusers and male victims in intimate relationships. These experiences illustrate the need for caution and careful listening to clearly discern what is happening in any particular situation. Despite these

---

3. Centers for Disease Control and Prevention (CDC), "Adverse childhood experiences (ACEs)," 2019, retrieved March 28, 2023, https://www.cdc.gov/violenceprevention/aces/index.html.

4. U.S. Department of Health and Human Services, Administration for Children and Families, Administration on Children, Youth and Families, Children's Bureau, "Child maltreatment 2019," (2021), https://www.acf.hhs.gov/sites/default/files/documents/cb/cm2019.pdf.

examples, however, we chose to use gender-specific language in this book for the following reasons:

1. *It is historically and statistically accurate.* Spousal abuse, domestic abuse, and intimate partner violence have historically referred to men using their strength, position, or power to coerce and control their female partners. When one mentions the term *domestic abuse*, the historically consistent image of the male abuser and female victim is present. This is important as it accurately represents the most frequent forms of domestic abuse we will encounter. We understand, for instance, that elder abuse refers to elderly folks being mistreated by a caregiver, and that child abuse refers to children being mistreated by a parent or guardian. We do not need to give caveats to those terms regarding the exceptions, unless of course we are speaking of a specific case in which a child has violated a guardian or an elderly person has hurt a caregiver.

   Women age eighteen to thirty-five remain at the highest risk of experiencing domestic abuse. According to the World Health Organization (WHO), 30 percent of women worldwide have experienced intimate partner violence (IPV) in their lifetime. Studies have consistently found that younger women are particularly vulnerable to IPV due to factors such as less relationship experience, less economic stability, and more exposure to risk-taking behaviors during this stage of their life.[5] IPV rates have decreased over time, but women still experience significantly higher rates of IPV than men.[6] Therefore, it's essential to recognize and address IPV as a significant

5. Ann L. Coker et al., "Physical and Mental Health Effects of Intimate Partner Violence for Men and Women," *American Journal of Preventive Medicine* (2011); World Health Organization, "Violence Against Women," (2017), https://www.who.int/news-room/fact-sheets/detail/violence-against-women.

6. Bureau of Justice Statistics, "Intimate Partner Violence, 1993–2010" (November 2012, revised September 29, 2015), chrome-extension://efaidnbmnnnibpcajpcglclefindmkaj/https://bjs.ojp.gov/content/pub/pdf/ipv9310.pdf.

public health issue that disproportionately affects women, particularly younger women.

2. *It is experientially accurate.* While I stated that we have all seen cases in which a woman has abused a man, it must be said that those cases are rare and often include unusual circumstances, such as a power dynamic that is unique to this couple. Additionally, male victims of female abuse tend to have far more resources available than their counterparts. This means that while the female abuser's behavior is harmful and must be addressed, concerns such as the male's long-term safety, escape, financial security, and available support systems are somewhat mitigated by the male partner's ability to leave, seek help, or receive counsel. Our experience reveals that women and children are the most vulnerable within the context of domestic abuse. Parts Two and Four of this book will go into further detail on women and children's unique vulnerabilities in domestic abuse situations and how to best minister to them.
3. *It is theologically consistent.* As someone who holds to complementarian theology, I have been somewhat surprised by the number of pastors and helpers who insist on mutualizing abuse within a relationship by claiming that the wife is unsubmissive or is perhaps provoking the abuse with her own sin patterns. While many churches make clear distinctions between men and women regarding leadership, teaching, and authority, those lines will often be blurred or softened when it comes to responsibility. Headship entails a hierarchy of responsibility; husbands must be called to account when wives are threatened, harmed, intimidated, or violated. If we acknowledge that husbands are the head of the house, then we must also recognize the potential to abuse that authority and hold them accountable when they do so. Part Three of this book will help you learn how to do this in a biblical way.

When Should We Involve the Civil Authorities?

There remains a great deal of confusion regarding helpers' responsibility to report accusations of abuse and a lack of understanding of how civil authorities such as law enforcement can respond. The simplest course of action would be to just require our staff or team to report any suspicion of abuse to the authorities, but is that what is best or what is required? This is where some additional research on your specific context is necessary:

1. *Know your state and local laws.* States have different reporting laws for clergy, counselors, and other helpers. Knowing your state and local laws will help you and your team have a baseline for mandated reporting as good Romans 13 citizens. Knowledge of state and local reporting laws will also help your team understand the importance of agency and safety when it comes to reporting other forms of abuse, such as child abuse, elder abuse, and abuse of the disabled.
2. *Know your options for legal protection.* Please understand that while all abuse is sinful, not all abuse is criminal. Law enforcement may not be prepared or able to intervene, so your report could leave the victim more vulnerable than before. Therefore, victim consent and safety planning are essential to reporting. Criminal abuse most often occurs when a threat or act of physical violence or the results of such is witnessed by law enforcement. Agencies around the country vary in their responses, and many officers will acknowledge the great difficulty in charging abusers with anything substantial. Having worked part-time in corrections with this population for twenty years, I can confirm that criminal abusers have often been given multiple chances by the court prior to being arrested or experiencing any significant consequences. Civil orders of protection may be a more reliable recourse for the victim to take, rather than pursuing criminal charges. Restraining

orders, protection orders, and the like establish a legal form of protection that entails consequences if violated.

Who Else Should Be Involved?

One of the models used by civil authorities with great success has been the Community Coordinated Response (CCR). The concept involves the collaboration of different agencies and stakeholders in a community to address domestic violence. For instance, when I served as a batterer intervention group facilitator, I also served on a CCR team that worked together on cases in the court system. This team included advocates, prosecutors, law enforcement, and others in the community who were involved in either the support of the victim or accountability for the perpetrator. Regardless of curriculum or services provided, the CCR was the most effective means of accountability as we could collaborate and share information vital to the case we were working on.

In this book, we argue for the benefits of a team approach to domestic abuse, and while we cannot recreate the CCR as we see in the court system, we have all experienced the benefits of a team-based approach even within the church. Teams will vary, of course, but having relationships with pastors, counselors, advocates, mentors, and others central to the care and confrontation needed in cases of domestic abuse aid each helper by providing lanes of care to serve within and added protection against collusion with the perpetrator.

The complexities of abuse require a sophisticated response. We rely on a diverse team of helpers in large part because we recognize that domestic abuse involves a wide variety of issues within a broad relational context; therefore, multiple helpers will serve the victim best. For instance, domestic abuse is a matter of justice, but not simply a matter of justice. Therefore, law enforcement responses alone are inadequate. The same could be said for healing, accountability, support, and care. Domestic abuse requires more than a therapeutic response, a pastoral response, an intervention, or advocacy.

What about Church Discipline?

Church discipline is a necessary part of addressing the sin of domestic abuse and promoting repentance and safety. In chapter 7, I discuss in further detail how to use the Matthew 18 model to carry out church discipline with an abusive person, but I'd like to highlight here a few things for you to consider when it comes to church discipline and domestic abuse.

1. *Abuse is divisive.* Paul instructs Titus in Titus 3:10 to warn a divisive person twice and then have nothing to do with them. Unrepentant abusers will often attempt to build allies and coalitions within the congregation in an attempt to build sides to a conflict rather than heed a warning from leaders who care. Individuals who spend time and energy opposing admonishment with attempts to create division among the leadership or within the congregation may in fact be confirming the need to finalize the church discipline process.
2. *Abuse that is especially violent, such as sexual assault, requires a prompt response.* In 1 Corinthians 5, the apostle Paul establishes a precedent for the immediate removal of those committing grievous relational sin. We suggest that sexual assault could warrant a more swift and decisive form of church discipline, including immediate removal, for the safety of the victim and the congregation.

What about Restoration?

As believers, we love to see restoration happen, but often when I am asked this question by leaders or helpers, it is almost always in reference to either restoring an abuser to their marriage or to a previously held ministry role. This makes sense because the gospel is central to our work—we believe in the good news that even the vilest among us can be made clean and that a wide variety of relationships can be restored. However, our primary focus for the abuser should be to restore their relationship with Christ, and we must keep in mind that sometimes restoration to other roles is not possible.

1. *Restoration to marriage and ministry is only possible if there is genuine repentance and change.* I have seen many men with willful, demanding hearts be transformed and display a willing spirit, acknowledging the harm they have done and accepting the consequences they now face. These men recognize that their acts of violence and abuse may have forfeited aspects of their life or livelihood, including loss of jobs, freedom, trust, and even marriage. Marriage reconciliation must always be preceded by genuine reconciliation to Christ. The assumption of spiritual shepherding roles must always be preceded by submission to the Good Shepherd. Chapter 10 (by Darby Strickland) will dive deeper into the careful work required to discern genuine repentance in abusers.
2. *Sometimes repentance leads to grieving the opportunities and relationships we squandered.* It is required of stewards to be found faithful (1 Corinthians 4:2) and abuses of position, authority, and power are acts of reckless stewardship. It will require a great deal of time and energy and grace to reestablish the trust that has been lost—if it ever happens. Counselors should prepare those they work with for the possibility that they may have to grieve the permanent loss of ministry positions they may be disqualified from or relationships they may have ruined.

We Are Praying for You

We often say that "prayer is the first work; it's not the only work, but it is the first work." So, will you pray? Will you pray for the wisdom needed to step into this difficult work, will you pray for those you will be caring for and those you will be confronting? Will you pray for the health of your church as you begin to work cases of domestic abuse, specifically for perseverance and strength to continue the hard work, knowing that you serve the only one capable of changing hearts and lives? Lastly, amid the controversies, the concerns, and the questions, I want you to know that we have prayed for you. Not that you would come to the exact same conclusions that we have, but that you and your team would engage in this work and do so from an informed, compassionate, and biblical perspective. We pray our words would be a catalyst for care among the hurting and vulnerable in your context.

CHAPTER 1

• • • •

Foundations of Domestic Abuse Care

Chris Moles

Domestic abuse may be among the most mismanaged and misunderstood issues facing the church today. A Lifeway Research poll of 1,000 pastors found that Protestant pastors want to be helpful when it comes to domestic abuse, but they often do not know where to start, and only half said they had any kind of plan to help a victim when they receive a disclosure of abuse.[1] To care for families well, it is imperative that biblical counselors, pastors, and other leaders within the church grow in their understanding of the complexities of family violence. Although this issue is not new to the church, it has more recently been reframed as a problem that we are directly called to speak into. At the same time, however, many church leaders feel ill-equipped to do so. My hope in this brief chapter is to answer, in part, two questions: How should the church help address the evil of domestic abuse, and how should pastors and biblical counselors best respond to domestic abuse?

1. LifeWay Research, "Domestic Violence and the Church," Research Report, sponsored by Autumn Miles, http://research.lifeway.com/wp-content/uploads/2017/02/Domestic-Violence-and-the-Church-Research-Report.pdf.

The Role of the Church

Although there are many specific roles that the church can play in addressing the problem of domestic abuse, there are two primary roles under which all of the other ones can be grouped. The church can address the evil of domestic abuse by (1) providing genuine, gospel-centered community, and (2) by teaching sound doctrine.

Provide gospel-centered community

The literature on domestic abuse typically includes among its best practices the important role that community can play in addressing the needs of both victims and abusers. Secular programs rely heavily on a coordinated response to address domestic violence within communities in which different agencies such as law enforcement, courts, victim advocates, batterer programs, and others work together to provide services and accountability and share information regarding compliance.[2] Similarly, the church in the context of domestic abuse can provide a form of gospel-centered community coordinated response in which victims are cared for and abusers are held accountable. The local church can provide resources and wise counsel for those suffering from abuse, continued discipleship for those progressively moving away from their abusive behaviors and attitudes, and discipline for those who obstinately remain in their sin. These are some of the broad ways in which the church can be a genuinely helpful community for domestic abuse situations. The next two chapters in this book will provide even more specific examples of how the church can be a light in the darkness of domestic abuse. Chapter 2 will give some guidance for how church leaders can discern whether or not abuse is happening when they are presented with a troubling situation within their congregation.

---

2. Ed Gondolf, *The Future of Batterer Programs: Reassessing Evidence-Based Practice*, U.S. Department of Justice, 2012, https://www.ojp.gov/ncjrs/virtual-library/abstracts/future-batterer-programs-reassessing-evidence-based-practice.

Teach sound doctrine

The second primary role that the church plays is to teach sound doctrine. Specifically, as it pertains to domestic abuse, the church must faithfully teach about the sufficiency of Scripture, the image of God in each person, the nature of relationships, and progressive sanctification.

The sufficiency of Scripture. Why is the sufficiency of Scripture such an important doctrine for domestic abuse? Because this doctrine maintains that the Scriptures speak to all human experiences, including domestic abuse. Bringing the insights of God's Word to bear on all kinds of counseling situations is the primary difference between biblical counselors and our secular counterparts. In the case of domestic abuse, holding to the sufficiency of the Scriptures allows us to bring the truth of God's love to the vulnerable, his compassion to the hurting, and his opposition to pride and violence to the oppressor. The Scriptures inform our beliefs about people, relationships, violence, and respect.

Unfortunately, however, many of us will have knee-jerk reactions to what our counselees disclose to us, and these instinctive responses might be shaped more by our church context or personal preferences and comfort than a reliance on the whole counsel of God's Word. For instance, if our upbringing or our church community strongly emphasizes the sacredness of the institution of marriage, then we may overlook what the Scriptures teach about the image-bearing nature of people. As a result, we may work hard to save a marriage at all costs, even to the neglect of the basic human needs of the people in the marriage.

Another area where it's essential that we allow the Scriptures to shape our understanding is in how we define violence. Some of us may have a very narrow view of violence, one that does not include categories like coercion or control. For example, Jesus instructs his followers in Matthew 5:39 to not resist an evil person, which we understand to mean not resist in kind or to return violence for violence. He then gives examples regarding how to respond to coercive control. Those examples include physical assault (turn the other cheek), using the system to coerce and rob (suing for your coat), as well as responding to oppressive laws that dehumanize individuals (go the extra mile).[3] If we only see violence as physical assault, then we may leave people in very volatile, hostile, and potentially deadly situations. Thus, the sufficiency of Scripture is a foundational doctrine for biblical counseling that the church must maintain and teach. It not only allows counselees to see how God speaks into their specific situations, but it also helps counselors guard against unbiblical beliefs in their own counsel.

The image of God. As I mentioned in the previous section, the image of God is another important doctrine that the church must faithfully preach to help address domestic abuse. When believers clearly understand that each person is made in the image of God, biblical counselors can help connect that doctrine to the problem of abuse. Assaulting another person physically, sexually, emotionally, or relationally is to violate or, as my friend Greg puts it, desecrate the image of God.[4] The belief that each person bears God's image can help both victims and abusers understand exactly how evil abuse really is.

The nature of relationships. Each person of the Trinity exists in perfect relationship with the other members of the Godhead. Because we are made in God's image, we are also inherently relational. We relate because God relates. The fact that God created us with a deeply embedded need for relationships can help us see that when we assault those we are in closest relationship with (our family), we're also damaging and assaulting the very way in which God designed us.

Furthermore, the church must not teach only about the origin and importance of relationships, but also what the Scriptures have

3. See Matthew 5:38–41. I realize that this passage has also been used to argue that victims of abuse should passively accept ill treatment, but a closer look at what Jesus is saying reveals that he is recommending ways to respond to evil with good (see also Romans 12:17–21). For a fuller discussion of this passage, see my blog post, "Resisting Abuse and Matthew 5," June 30, 2019, http://www.chrismoles.org/news/2018/2/25/resisting-abuse-and-matthew-chapter-5-a6s5l.

4. Jeremy Pierre and Greg Wilson, *When Home Hurts: A Guide for Responding Wisely to Domestic Abuse in Your Church* (Fearn, Scotland: Christian Focus, 2021).

to say about how we are to behave within those relationships. Abuse violates the revealed will of God because God gives directives to husbands and wives that forbid abusive behavior. God is very clear in his Word about how husbands in particular are to treat their wives in ways that preclude abuse. Ephesians 5:25 commands husbands to "love your wives, as Christ also loved the church and gave himself up for her" and a few verses later says that "husbands should love their wives as their own bodies" (v. 28). Colossians 3:19 exhorts, "Husbands, love your wives, and do not be harsh with them." First Peter 3:7a commands husbands to "live with your wives in an understanding way."

Progressive sanctification. The doctrine of progressive sanctification is foundational to biblical counseling in general, but it has particular implications for domestic abuse situations. Simply put, the doctrine of progressive sanctification teaches that as people are redeemed, they are called and empowered to change, to pursue holiness. To provide pastoral care is to call people back to the Scriptures for guidance and simultaneously help them learn how to rely on the power and presence of the Holy Spirit to change, grow, endure, trust, hope, and, dare I say, live.

But in situations of domestic abuse, the doctrine of progressive sanctification specifically allows us to call victims to find continued healing and growth in Christ. The abuse they have suffered is not the end of their story. I will admit that working consistently with domestic abuse for nearly twenty years has taken its toll on me. It can be difficult and discouraging work. At the same time, there are few joys greater than seeing a victim recover her voice, her life, and herself.

In the early days of this work, I was pastoring a very small church (I still do for that matter), but at this time we had no facilities, and the church phone was my cell phone. It was not uncommon for victims of domestic abuse to find the church number and call me looking for help or comfort. It was difficult time in ministry, but also a rewarding time as I spent many afternoons and evenings on the front porch of our small home listening, praying, and attempting to serve the hurting person on the other side of the call. I met one of these precious ladies shortly after our phone call at an event. There we picked up where we left off, crying and praying and trying to connect her to services. I recall that her hurt was so deep that I later described her to my wife as a shell of a person. It was years before I heard from her again, this time at an event I was speaking at. She waited patiently in the line to ask questions. I greeted her, and she reminded me of the time we had spent on the phone, and later in person. I was undone. This couldn't be the same person—her smile, her face, her voice. I was meeting someone new, someone healed, someone changed by the power of God. I had to take a seat as we cried together again, but this time celebrating what only our God could do. These stories are more and more common in my work, and I praise God for the occasional reminders through the life of abuse survivors.

The church's belief in and commitment to progressive sanctification gives us a powerful and needed voice in this important work. The harm that has been done to victims of abuse cannot be erased in a day, but by the power of the Spirit, damaged lives can be restored. In addition, progressive sanctification gives us hope for those who have abused. The doctrine of progressive sanctification compels us to call abusers to repentance, transformation, and continued discipleship. Without a doubt, the root of domestic abuse resides within the heart of an abusive individual. While we strive to serve both the victim and the abuser, we acknowledge that the cause of the abuse must be addressed thoroughly by calling the abuser to repentance, accountability, and continued discipleship. I have yet to see an effective remedy to the problem of domestic abuse that does not include holding the abuser responsible and accountable for the abuse. The doctrine of progressive sanctification not only compels us to do this, but it also sustains us in persevering when change and growth seem slow.

The Response of Biblical Counselors

While the church as a whole has a role to play in addressing domestic abuse, biblical counselors are the members of the body of Christ who have been specifically called and equipped to respond to domestic abuse. Pastors, elders, deacons, lay leaders, and vocational biblical counselors can do much to help victims and confront abusers. We represent an army of compassionate helpers that, with the proper training, can serve on the front line of loving, gospel-centered responses to the great harm being done to and within families.

A framework for response: 1 Thessalonians 5:14

Much of what biblical counselors do in domestic abuse intervention and prevention is encapsulated in 1 Thessalonians 5:14. It not only describes our work, it also guides us as we aim to do this work well: "Now we exhort you, brethren, warn those who are unruly, comfort the fainthearted, uphold the weak, be patient with all" (NKJV). Each of these commands is rich with implications for domestic abuse situations. Let us begin at the end of the verse by considering what it means to "be patient with all" when we enter into a domestic abuse situation.

Be patient with everyone. A good starting point in responding to the wickedness of domestic abuse within the walls of the church is to create an atmosphere of patient care. Paul directs the church to be patient with every believer, but this is far more difficult in cases of domestic abuse than you may think. Unfortunately, it is easy to become impatient with this work. Biblical counselors and pastors may lose patience with victims who do not make decisions as quickly as the helper desires, or who hesitate to heed counsel due to the many pressures they are experiencing as well as potential consequences associated with each possible decision. Abusers may test the patience of helpers through attempts to manipulate, threaten, collude, or intimidate those involved in holding them accountable. I have heard many stories of pastors or biblical counselors who rushed through the process because they wanted a quick resolution to the problem.

Being impatient can lead to superficial solutions that revictimize a victim. The process of understanding a domestic abuse situation and pursuing real change requires a great deal of time because there are many slow-moving and complex parts. But when counselors are patient, they might experience pushback to their approach. This can take the form of questions about how quickly the relationship can be restored, or how soon the boundaries can be removed. But these questions often do not have easy answers. The patient counselor must carefully consider, *How can we best care for the victim? How can we best and safely confront the abuser? How can we best honor God and the testimony of Christ?* Friends, quick resolution tends to be sloppy, and it can place people in further danger. We want to foster a patient atmosphere of care. So, as we consider the kinds of individuals Paul addresses in this passage, it is imperative that we maintain and practice patience, as well as encourage our counselees to be patient with the process.

Warn the unruly. The first category Paul addresses is the unruly or idle individual; he calls the church to warn or admonish these members of the church. The unruly person encapsulates the types of men that I've worked with over the years, which have included those who are incredibly passive to the point of neglect and those who are aggressive to the point of abuse. Both require a response that includes admonishment or warning. Our role is to patiently confront the choices, behaviors, and heart motivations that have caused harm to their families. I'm not saying you must be mean or attempt to control the man yourself; in a later chapter, I will discuss the Galatians 6 call to gentle confrontation. It is important that we say hard things in safe and winsome ways. Nonetheless, those hard things *have* to be said because there are a group of people among us who are doing harm to their partners, and that requires admonition. One of the greatest ways we can reduce the abuse happening in our midst is by confronting abusers, calling them to repentance, providing consistent accountability, and pursuing continued discipleship or discipline.

Comfort the fainthearted. Believers engaged in soul care are also called to comfort the fainthearted. Some people among us are discouraged. In fact, we hear a repeated refrain from victims who contact our ministries: they desperately want their church and their church leadership to understand what they're going through, but they feel alone and hopeless and broken within and by the church. Biblical counselors and other church leaders must speak words of comfort to folks who are discouraged. I hope you find encouragement in the chapters that follow as you learn more about various ways you can care for those hurt through the sin of domestic abuse. Frankly, sometimes the only choices in front of a victim are less than desirable choices. She may be walking through the most difficult, desperate, and lonely time of her life. Family members, friends, employers, coworkers, and others will feel defeated and discouraged in the face of such desperate circumstances. Many times we too will feel helpless in the face of all the trouble our counselees are facing, but a word of encouragement, an act of kindness, or simply being present with them may be exactly what they need in any given moment.

Uphold the weak. Weak is a difficult word to use to describe someone, at least in our present world. Sometimes when church leaders or biblical counselors use the term *weak*, it can be misunderstood as indicating that we believe victims are weak-minded, or frail, or less than. The idea here is not an indictment on the individual's character, but rather a call for us to step into their circumstances and suffering. Paul seems to be instructing us to hold onto those who are suffering, and, when possible, to hold off the evil being done to them. Weakness describes the state or position they are in—they are weak because they are being oppressed by the abusive use of power. We have a multifaceted call—within our patient atmosphere of care, we must confront the abuser, speak comfort to the sufferer, and hold onto the vulnerable while holding off the assault of the oppressive. Biblical counselors represent a unique category of helper that may bridge the gap between the hope the gospel speaks of with the safety the church can provide.

The Importance of Humility

Biblical counselors and other church leaders who provide pastoral care bring gifts, tools, and expertise to the complex problem of domestic abuse. However, while biblical counseling is a response to abuse, it is not the only response. It is important that we maintain a posture of humility that recognizes our weaknesses. Some potential blind spots for those who provide biblical counsel may include not knowing when to involve the government and not drawing on the expertise of those who have specialized in domestic abuse care and intervention. Being willing to learn and to call for help when needed are essential aspects of biblical counsel in general, but especially in the complex and potentially dangerous context of domestic abuse.

Involving the government

Romans 13 reminds us that the government serves as an agent of God's wrath, and as such, they wield the sword. While not all domestic abuse is criminal, there is much that falls within the purview of civil authorities. We recommend that anyone who provides pastoral care know their state and local reporting laws. Please do not assume anything—ask questions of human service professionals and law enforcement. State laws vary on mandated reporting, and failing to involve the proper authorities opens you up to be potentially liable for negligence, not to mention leaving the victim in a dangerous situation. Understand reporting laws, establish a safety plan, obtain training in assessing a person's dangerousness and lethality, and become versed in your community's civil orders of protection procedures to be a humble Romans 13 partner.

Pursuing wisdom and insight

The vast majority of biblical counselors and pastors are trained to be generalists—they are the family doctor of care and counseling. This has been a healthy strategy as we aim to serve a wide variety of people and problems, as well as avoid some of the pitfalls of professionalism.

However, there is much to be said about case volume and the case wisdom that can develop out of an intense focus and exposure. We must not assume that our training and experience have adequately prepared us to know how to properly respond to cases of domestic abuse. There is much to be learned from folks who have spent significant amounts of time with this population, whether they are biblical counselors, like the authors of this book, or secular experts who have made tremendous, common-grace observations based on their countless hours of work.

My prayer is that the church of Jesus Christ will be the safest place on the planet for women and children. I pray that the church will lead the way in not only providing compassionate care, but also in developing best practices to address the needs of victims and confront the abusers. We represent an army of responders who can effectively, graciously, compassionately, and firmly confront the evil of domestic abuse. As we do so, we will simultaneously promote healthy, God-honoring relationships.

CHAPTER 2

....

The Church's Response to Domestic Abuse

Kirsten Christianson

Ed Welch helps us understand the importance of the church's response to domestic violence:

> Domestic anger and violence deserve our immediate attention, even when there is only a mere hint of a problem. . . Although the state can certainly help when women are victimized by their husband's anger, the church must respond and take action. God hates injustice. This might be one of the few times when those who help are called to righteous indignation. Men, and even women, err in underestimating how difficult it can be to live with an angry spouse.[1]

Isaiah 1:17 exhorts the church to "Learn to do good; seek justice, *correct oppression*; bring justice to the fatherless, plead the widow's cause" (emphasis added). In fact, over and over again throughout the Old Testament, God condemns oppression. From the beginning, God had a plan to rescue us from oppression in all its forms: our own sin, sins committed against us, and the (temporary) deeds of the evil one—that plan is Jesus. At the beginning of his ministry in Luke 4,

1. Edward T. Welch, "Counseling Problems and Procedures," Lecture 2, CCEF School of Biblical Counseling, https://www.ccef.org/course/counseling-problems-procedures/.

Jesus said that he came to "set at liberty those who are oppressed" (v. 18). Because our Christian life is one of being conformed to his image, of course we want to follow his example. But how do we engage with oppression in our local church?

Let's start by considering a few questions: What if the church—*your* church—endeavored to stop domestic abuse and to address the physical, spiritual, and emotional needs *of the abused and the abuser with the hope of healing and restoration*? What if your church's primary concern was for the soul of each person trapped in a destructive cycle of abuse?

This chapter is a little different from the others. It is a plea from my heart to the reader, particularly to church leaders—pastors, elders, and deacons—who desire to shepherd the flock among you. My desire in this chapter is to encourage you undershepherds as you seek to minister in a complex, confusing, time-consuming, and redemptive ministry. I want to help you think through how to address domestic abuse in your church *in a biblically faithful, organizationally sustainable, and practically helpful way.* By the end of this chapter, my prayer is that you will have some tools to begin recognizing and responding to domestic abuse for the strengthening of the church, her people, and their families.

For the counselors who are reading, *please keep reading.* If you are seeing abused or abusive believers in your practice, most likely they attend or are members of a church. By reading this book, you will have a sharper picture of how you can help church leaders shepherd their people from your seat on the bus. Your understanding of a vision and process allows you to serve your counselee by helping the pastor(s) minister knowledgeably and wisely.

These topics are extremely important. Abuse, oppression, or destructive relational patterns—whatever you want to call these chronic, intractable, besetting, deeply entrenched ways of mistreatment that happen within the covenantal marital relationship—require that we develop good theological frameworks and address these issues with love, reason, and conviction. Proverbs reminds us that there is no such thing as cookie-cutter ministry. "Answer not a fool . . . answer a fool . . ." (Proverbs 26:4–5).

The church (including me) needs to grow in the skill of Pauline conversation: listening to understand, speaking the truth in love, letting ministry help us read Scripture, and making sure ministry is rooted in Scripture. Paul equips us in Ephesians 4:25–32 with great tools for productive conversations and one-another care.

The Biggest Question

I am going to address what is probably the most-asked question first: *How do I know it is abuse?*

This is a difficult question, and it's easy to not want to step into a situation because you are afraid you don't know the answers. The biggest roadblock to wise domestic abuse ministry is *fear*: fear of the topic; fear that the ways of the world are creeping into the church; fear of the complexities of private, intimate relational sins; fear of getting it wrong; fear of getting it right; of the impact on church relationships; fear of disagreement; or fear of missing something. And these are just a few fears!

But remember Paul's words to Timothy, "For God gave us a spirit not of fear but of power and love and self-control" (2 Timothy 1:7). Fruitful ministry starts with faith-filled, encouraged ministers. God's people don't run from hard things. Because the Lord helps us, we—like Jesus—set our faces like flint (Isaiah 50:7). You have the God of the universe who has given you everything you need for "life and godliness" (2 Peter 1:3) in your ministry to God's people. His gifts include the Word (preached, taught, read, and lived), the empowerment of the Spirit, the example of the ministry life of Jesus, and a willing heart. Take heart!

Don't Miss the Signs

You *are* going to encounter these ministry situations if you haven't already. In fact, you probably already have, even if you don't know it.

It's easy to miss, and one of the biggest reasons is that it is *exceedingly rare* for a woman to present with the words "I am being abused by my husband." Uttering these words provokes feelings of deep shame and fear. There are several reasons for this.

First, most believing wives do not want to speak of their husbands in disrespectful ways. The Bible teaches that wives are to respect their husbands, and women who take those words to heart (which are most women in the pew) are also the ones least likely to want to disrespect him by exposing his sin to others. In Bible study, women are reticent to share hard marriage dynamics for fear that they may be gossiping. By the time a woman reveals that something abnormal is going on in the home, she has read many marriage books, studied how to be a more godly wife, floated ambiguous questions in smaller group settings, and tried countless ways to be a better wife and mom. Most women do not want a divorce. *Most women in the church want God-honoring marriages and deeply desire to respect and love their husbands.*

Second, very few believing women understand what is happening when they experience oppression. They find it very difficult and heartbreaking to consider what is happening to them. It feels shameful to share being repeatedly called words that we can't print in this book, being shouted at nose to nose, or relentlessly and wrongfully accused of always dishonoring God or having bad motives toward her husband. *How can this be happening to me?* she thinks. *I love him! I am trying to love him better.*

This means that when she finally gets the courage to talk to someone, she often can't tell a linear story, and she will tend to focus more on her own sin than what she is experiencing. She will most often present with tears and despair, be defensive of her husband, seem confused, and express a deep desire to honor God in her marital relationship. (As a side note, it is not unusual for a friend or small group member to reach out on behalf of a woman or a couple in a hard or painful marriage. In these kinds of marriages, often people have tried to help with advice and counsel, but it has not borne fruit. So they reach out to a pastor or staff member to ask for help and/or resources.)

Guiding Principles for Helpers

While the purpose of this chapter is to help church leaders consider what they need to think through in order to identify and address domestic abuse in their particular church, let me just offer the following six guiding principles to help you care well when a woman first seeks you out:

1. *Listen compassionately and wisely and invite her to bring a friend or have another woman in the room.* Few elders really understand that it takes a lot of courage for most people to talk to elders about things that aren't going so well. So as she shares, keep in mind that there are a lot of thoughts and emotions coursing through her.
2. *Reassure her that you are hearing her and are leaning in.* Saying, "I hear you and I am continuing to listen," lays the ground for providing wise, protective counsel while allowing you to gather the necessary information you need to minister well.
3. *Ask clarifying questions so that you have a good understanding of what she is sharing.* In this first meeting, you are asking good questions that help both you and her understand her situation better, as Jesus did over and over again. *This is where you want to assess whether there is danger to anyone in the home.* Have there been threats or actual physical violence? Have resources been cut off? Have children been harmed?
4. *Minister to her.* Let her know that you are glad she came for help—it's what congregants are supposed to do when they are in deep waters! Stop and pray with her. Whatever is going on—whether or not it's on the spectrum of abuse—something is wrong and she needs help. Consider using the questions in appendix A on page 202 to help her accurately share what life is like in her home. See chapter 4 to better understand the abuse victim is experiencing.
5. *Collaborate with her to decide helpful next steps.* Does she want you to reach out to her husband? Does she need a referral

for wise, trained counseling? Work together to identify and articulate the next several steps. (This is where the friend with her can be particularly helpful.)

6. *Communicate clearly what help you are offering, who you will be sharing information with, and what level of information you will share.* These are intimate details of her life and marriage, and care should be taken with them. Console her and pray with her again.

With all of this in mind, I have broken up this chapter into two sections. The first section addresses how to assess various aspects of your church if you are to even recognize domestic abuse in your congregation's marriages. You will need to consider your church's leadership, structure, culture, and resources. The second section discusses how to choose a model and approach for responding to abuse when it is identified.

Part 1: Laying a Foundation: Church Leadership, Structure, Culture, and Resources

Sustainable, helpful ministry always begins with identifying the need. Here we have identified the need—the church needs to recognize and respond biblically to oppression in marriages and families. In this case, meeting that need will include

- securing like-minded leadership;
- assessing your church's structure, culture, and resources;
- creating a process and a plan for implementation (always with a willingness to be flexible); and
- practicing humility.

This section addresses the first two bullet points: securing like-minded leadership and assessing your church's structure, ethos, and resources. As we lay this foundation for effective ministry, keep in mind that overpromising and underproducing hurts people. Unaligned elders harry the flock. Take the time to build a strong foundation so that you can be truly helpful to suffering and struggling members of your congregation.

Securing like-minded leadership

I cannot overstate how critical like-minded, bought-in leadership is to wise domestic abuse ministry in the church. *This is key.* I purposely use the word *like-minded* because God gives different convictions and sensibilities, and that is a gift to the process, *but* there absolutely has to be an overarching agreed-upon definition of abuse, a shared commitment to addressing it in believing marriages, and a clear, coordinated process. To foster unity, here are some things for leaders to consider as they contemplate ministering to oppressive marriages:

- First, it's important to discover the particular needs of your church. How are marriages doing in your flock? What are you doing in your church to (1) prepare engaged couples for marriage (including assessing for relational flags); and (2) strengthening existing marriages in the body? Is your counseling ministry full of hard, broken marriages? Are you aware of domestic abuse in your church? Do you wonder what you may be missing?
- Second, creating unity—shared definitions, vision, and conviction—will take many candid conversations during a period of six months to a year. Are you willing to invest the time to learn and discern an appropriate church ministry response?
- Are candid conversations taking place among the leaders in which elders can speak their minds, disagree, and continue to come to the table to find God's path forward?
    - What are the theological and philosophical differences?[2]
    - Can you find real, on-the-ground unity (rather than just on paper)?

2. Andrew David Naselli and J. D. Crowley, *Conscience: What It Is, How to Train It, and Loving Those Who Differ* (Wheaton, IL: Crossway, 2016). This book is indispensable for helping elders and church members consider how to work through their different approaches to the various ministry issues that present in the church.

- Do the elders trust each other? When the overseeing elders substantiate abuse, will the other elders trust him so that care for the couple can proceed in appropriate ways? Disagreements halfway through the process make life really hard for the families in your care.
- Are there enough elders to care effectively for the size of your congregation?
- Are elders expected to give or oversee congregational care? If not the elders, who will be entrusted with this ministry?
- Will every elder be involved in domestic abuse care? Or will you delegate to elders who are trained and have the required competencies?

After the elders have come to a place of like-mindedness and are ready to move forward, you will want to be realistic about the varying gifts of those you are involving in the ministry. I have worked with elders in many churches across the United States. Elders, like the rest of us, have differing competencies, strengths, weaknesses, and struggles. Their role as elders doesn't negate that they are human beings. They are called to be above reproach, but they cannot be sinless. They also cannot fill all the roles needed in a domestic abuse case. Biblically, elders are not required to have the same skill set as professional counselors or domestic abuse experts. They are called to shepherd the flock among them. There are many ways to do that—and it is a demanding calling. Elders are required to apply the Word of God to all areas of life, which includes how husbands and wives relate to one another. Elders can draw on the gifts, training, and expertise of others to provide the intensive counseling, accountability, and practical help that domestic abuse cases require.

Over the last thirty years that I have worked with elders in various churches, it has been enlightening to see the breadth and depth of what they are called to enter into on a day-to-day basis as ministers of the church. In a flock of 500, there can easily be 600 opinions on how some issue should be addressed in the church (do we mask or do we not?). Given how confusing domestic abuse is for everyone involved, when a situation comes to light in a congregation, the elders are going to hear thoughts and opinions from all sides. In order to prevent division, they need to have ongoing conversations throughout the duration of their involvement with an abusive marriage. This is critical to maintain like-mindedness. I am thankful for elders who want to shepherd their congregants with love, wisdom, and unity.

Assessing church structure and resources

After developing like-mindedness, the next step is to assess your church's structure and resources. It is bad care when a church overpromises and underproduces. Be realistic about the level of support you can offer and maintain. The following questions are intended to help guide you in this process:

- How thin are your resources already spread? What is the congregant-to-pastor ratio in your church? How many members does each elder oversee? Where have you noticed being stretched already? Is long-term care something your leadership structure does well?
- What depth of care are you able to provide to congregants? Consider financial assistance, practical help, discipleship, counseling, etc.
- Where will domestic abuse care fit in your church ministry structure? Will it be its own ministry? Will it be a ministry of the deacons? Will be it an arm of the counseling ministry?
- How does accountability work in your church?
    - How do you measure quality of ministry?
    - In what ways do you assure that ministry is progressing?
    - Who is in charge of catching when care has stalled out or mistakes have been made—even well-intentioned mistakes?
- Are you one campus or multicampus?
    - Will the ministry be centrally overseen or will it be unique to each campus? How will you ensure a standard of care?

- Who will provide on-the-ground care?
  - Will you need to hire more staff or reallocate resources?
  - Who will coordinate the care team?
  - Who will provide administrative help?
- How will you engage different small groups and Bible study leaders?
- Is your church resourced enough to provide a robust domestic abuse ministry or do you need to refer portions out once there is a report?
- Does your church have community relationships with social service and law enforcement agencies? If not, reach out to local domestic violence shelters, batterer intervention agencies, child protection services, and local law enforcement agencies to become familiar with what they offer. They are usually delighted to hear that a church is getting involved and willing to partner with them.
- How does your church engage volunteers in ministry?
  - Are there congregants who have special gifts, talents, and/or vocations (police, lawyers, social workers, counselors) to help form your church's domestic abuse ministry?
- What are your church's weaknesses? A domestic abuse ministry will expose the cracks—and that's a blessing!

Assessing the church's culture of care

In Galatians 6:2, we are called to "[b]ear one another's burdens, and so fulfill the law of Christ." The ESV study note says "To bear one another's burdens is the supreme imitation of Jesus, the ultimate burden-bearer." The Greek word for *bear* means to support or pick up. When considering domestic abuse ministry, here are some foundational questions to help your church or organization assess how your church is doing in bearing one another's burdens. The questions are organized to categorize leadership concerns and congregational concerns.

Leadership

- Does the care structure in your church actually function? Historically, has your church moved from having initiatives to carrying out the planned ministries?
- If you rely on small groups to be the first line of care for members, do the small group leaders know this expectation, and does it actually happen? Are they equipped for the hard situations that make up the realities of our lives?
  - Do married couples have the opportunity to work on the hard things that come up in their relationships? Do small group leaders disciple couples through conflict? Are there people that are skilled to help a couple navigate differences, such as financial management, roles in the marriage, and parenting philosophies?
- How does your church leadership define *care*? Is there a threshold at which point care needs to be referred out? What does the leadership believe the commitment to church members looks like in times of crisis?
- What role does counseling play in care at your church? Is that ministry the first line of care? Or is it one aspect of congregational care?
- Have you educated those involved in crisis care so that they know they feel equipped and are supported as they provide the help they are tasked to give? In other words, if caregivers become overwhelmed or burdened, do they know where they can go to receive ministry for themselves?
  - In chronic crisis situations, like domestic abuse, caregivers (pastors, deacons, disciplers, counselors, small group members) often become overwhelmed and feel unequipped and inadequate. This may lead to burnout and fading away, leaving those in crisis alone, hurt, and worse off than before they started with your ministry.

- Are there care resources for our caregivers? In other words, if caregivers become overwhelmed or burdened, do they know where they can go for ministry for themselves?
  - Do you have a way to care for all of those affected by a couple struggling in their marriage? It can be very hard on family, small group members, and close friends.
  - Caregivers are not ministering in a vacuum. They have families, struggles, and busy schedules. Sometimes crises come up for them. It's important to check in with caregivers beyond asking, "How are you doing? Oh, good!" Good questions include:
    - How is your marriage? Are you prioritizing your spouse?
    - How are your kids doing? Do they feel like they see you enough?
    - Where are you getting your nurturing? Do you have friends and/or small group members who know you are involved in a taxing ministry and who pray for you regularly?

Congregational

- Do members bear the fruit of the Spirit by practicing the one-another commands with each other? Do your congregants truly know one other?
- Do you have an identified care stream? Ask a congregant, "If you found out tomorrow that you had cancer, or you were experiencing major suffering, do you know how to reach out for prayer and practical support in our church?"
  - How do you, or will you, determine what level of care to provide to someone reaching out for help? Would you base it upon membership or attendance? Or is your care open to the broader community?
- Do people feel free to ask for help of any kind, such as financial help, crisis care, meals, help navigating disputes, etc.? Do

you receive requests for help, or have you received feedback that people didn't know how to get care your church offers?

- What are the church members' expectations of care from the church? Do the expectations match church resources?
    - If your church has a document that lays out expectations and promises between shepherds and congregants, are you carrying out your obligations to the congregation?
        - How would domestic abuse care fit into the document? For instance, when separation is on the table, how will shepherding unfold? Do congregants need pastoral approval?
- Is there a shared understanding between the leadership and the congregation of what constitutes a crisis and what kind of care will be provided? For instance,
    - Some crises call for prayer, some meals, and others community check-ins. Care is going to be for a shorter duration.
    - Other crises are more chronic and sinful in nature. Congregants who have become ensnared or hurt by sin may need protection and/or accountability. Care is going to be ongoing for a longer period of time.
- Do your church members have a biblical, healthy understanding of what bearing one another's burdens means? Do they know what it does not mean?

Part 2: Creating a Model and a Process

Whole-family domestic abuse care requires wisdom, patience, discernment, and a well-defined model and process. The process needs to be clear enough that everyone knows what is happening and what to expect, and facile enough that it can flex with the particularities of each presenting situation. Each situation is made up of at least two people made in the image of God, with all that entails. Each person comes with their own family history, strengths, weaknesses, and sin-struggles, which means that walking them through the process is going to look different with each situation.

Model

I recommend a team-based approach, which you will see in chapter 3. I have worked with churches in which the pastor or a very small elder board or session is trying to do everything on their own. They quickly become overwhelmed, divided, or burned out—or all three! With a team, you are sharing the ministry work, drawing on wider gifting and experience, and facilitating the coordination of care of both spouses. Proverbs 11:14 states, "Where there is no guidance, a people falls, but in an abundance of counselors there is safety." This is true for everyone involved. In particular, I believe it is important to have the following team members and considerations that allow cooperation:

- *At least two elders.* Domestic abuse situations take many hours and an abundance of wisdom. It's wise and sharpening to have differing perspectives because it will be the elder board that moves forward with decisions surrounding separation, divorce, and/or discipline.
- *A discipler or mentor or advocate for each person.* This is a person who will help them process the care and input they are receiving and continue to point them toward Jesus, their first and best Advocate.
- *A counselor for each person (including any children in the family).* Each counselor will establish appropriate counseling goals with the help of the rest of the team.
- *Releases of Information (ROI) for everyone on the team.* This allows pertinent information to be shared so that the counseling and encouragement can be more robust, rather than offered in a vacuum. The terms of the ROIs must be thoroughly explained to everyone on the team.
- *Confidentiality is absolutely critical.* In the early days of care, when safety issues are unknown, the circle of people involved

needs to remain small. It can be enlarged as necessary, if the team so determines.

Other team members may include community partnerships. Even though these voices (Child Protective Services, attorneys, and police) may not be coming from believers, they have a lot of experience and often can be a great help. It is important to establish good communication and trust. I have found that community agencies are astounded that the church will get involved, and they are very thankful for our help. At the same time, remember to stay in your lane. The church team should not give legal counsel or interfere with criminal or child protective services investigations.

Process: The gift of Matthew 18

A wise, articulated process means that everyone will work from the same page to provide sound biblical care. When responding to domestic abuse, the church is tasked with many things: receiving a complaint, verifying the complaint, addressing sin, and supporting a sufferer. I have seen churches handle this in different ways, including having no process, using an elder-exclusive process, referring all of it out, or scrambling to keep up with the demands of a complex marital situation.

I'll quickly sketch out one possibility below; however, answering the assessment questions should inform what kind of process you create for your particular church setting. For instance, if you only have two elders because you are a small church, and you have two or more marital abuse situations, you will quickly find you do not have the time, bandwidth, and other resources to shepherd the couples without more help. If you have a multicampus church, you will need to think through whether domestic abuse ministry is going to look the same on each campus or if it will need to flex due to different contexts. Or if you are in a church that does not practice discipline, it will be incumbent upon you to think through how you will establish what is happening in the marriage and what accountability and help you will offer. Another dilemma that you will have to sort out is if one is a member, and the other is not.

Because what I propose below is taken directly from the Bible, I think this approach will provide you with an excellent foundation from which you can craft your own domestic abuse ministry process, which will be biblical, sustainable, and practically helpful. I believe using Matthew 18 is helpful because it articulates from the start what the expectations are: hearing that leads either to repentance and eventual reconciliation or unrepentance and removal from the church. If either the husband or the wife is not a church member, you may still use the process, but discipline for the offending nonmember will be off the table. However, the process still allows you to confront and offer consequences (such as supporting separation, and in cases of physical abuse, utilizing civil orders of protection and the like).

The other reason I believe Matthew 18 is helpful is that it provides the offended wife a biblical way to expose sin. In a believing marriage, husband, and wife are also brother and sister in Christ, which means all of the relational one-anothers are in operation in the marital relationship. As we come alongside her, we want her to understand that she is biblically warranted to bring her husband's sin to him. She doesn't need permission from the elders. (However, if there is a question of safety, punishment, or retribution, she can ask the elder for help.) The biblical, Matthew 18 response restores the voice she has in Christ *and* adds the weight of gospel reconciliation to the process.

This is important because an abusive husband often treats his wife as though she is not a full member of the body of Christ (and through his treatment tempts her to believe this lie). Second Timothy 3:6–7 talks about women who are "burdened with [their own] sins and led astray by various passions, always learning and never able to arrive at a knowledge of the truth." Abused women are often *like* these women in that they focus more on their own sins, trying to be better and do better, and minimize or even justify the pattern of sin they are experiencing from their husband. They listen to his false teaching (e.g.,

"You are subservient to me" or "You cannot talk to anyone else about what is happening in our marriage") that distorts how God meant for a marriage to depict Christ and the church, and neglects the truth of what is really happening in their marriage. Tempted to turn from the Lord and take refuge in other passions—things like making their children their entire life, or becoming very angry and resentful, etc.—they forget that they are to be a helpmeet to their husband. As a godly wife, they are able to exhort as well as encourage their husbands—respectfully, with love, for God's glory and their good.

Matthew 18 makes clear that when we believe Jesus, we are called to bring unrepentant sin to each other, and Paul doesn't exclude wives and husbands. An abused wife who approaches her husband in this way is acting faithfully in obedience to Christ, for the good of her marriage and the glory of God. Matthew 18:15–17 exhorts us,

> "If your brother sins against you, go and tell him his fault, between you and him alone. If he listens to you, you have gained your brother. But if he does not listen, take one or two others along with you, that every charge may be established by the evidence of two or three witnesses. If he refuses to listen to them, tell it to the church. And if he refuses to listen even to the church, let him be to you as a Gentile and a tax collector."

This passage provides a wise process for everyone involved in a domestic abuse situation to follow. Everyone has a voice, protection, due process, and a clear outcome based on personal responses. It reveals fruit.

It's important to remember that while the Matthew 18 process takes up just six verses in the Bible, it will often take months (or possibly a couple of years) to complete. Below, I provide a sketch of how it could look. First, a caveat (although I could provide many): there is not one prescribed way to walk out Matthew 18. This is just *a* way to show how it could be done.

Keep in mind that if you decide to follow Matthew 18, that by the time a woman reaches out for help, she most often—and I mean 99.9 percent of the time—has already done verse 15: "If your brother sins against you, go and tell him his fault, between you and him alone. If he listens to you, you have gained your brother." By the time she shows up in your office, she has pleaded with her husband to discontinue his sinful behavior or asked for them to go to marriage counseling (which is unhelpful if there is abuse), or has gone to a lot of marriage counseling, or has asked if they could speak to an elder, etc. Usually he has turned her down, and that is why she is sitting in front of you.

One final word before we walk this out: If you uncover sexual sin in the safety assessment, it would be wise to rethink your process and consider 1 Corinthians 5. If you uncover physical danger, threats of physical danger, or if housing or finances have been threatened or been removed, you will need to ensure safety and protection for the wife and children and probably speed up the process.

Meet Mary

Mary reaches out to the counseling pastor for help with her marriage. Pastor Don takes the call, and during the intake, several flags come up as he listens to what she is reporting. She has no access to their money. Her husband berates her, and when she tries to ask for a break or escapes to the bathroom, he stands at the door and screams at her. She shares that he wakes her in the middle of the night for sex at least four times a week. She wants counseling so that she can work on these things to have a better, more peaceful, marriage. The pastor asks her to come in and meet with him and a female ministry partner to hear more about what she is experiencing.

Pastor Don and his ministry partner, Brittany, meet with Mary and the small group leaders, who share their observations of the husband's treatment of Mary. Pastor Don and Brittany ask questions to gain clarity and discern more of what is happening in the marriage. Mary's safety is also assessed at that time, and any necessary plans are made for protection. There will certainly be a referral for individual counseling. If there is concern that abuse is present, marital counseling will be tabled while they gather more information.

At the end of the ninety minutes, Pastor Don asks Mary if she has addressed these sinful behaviors with her husband. He will take the time to thoroughly explain Matthew 18:15–20, helping her see how the Bible has laid out a path for her to appeal to her husband to repent, and if her husband won't, to gather one or two witnesses to address his sin patterns in the marriage. Pastor Don will clearly take her through what the process could look like in her particular marriage.

Pastor Don will then ask her how she wants to move forward. Does she want to take some time to pray on her own and with her small group leaders? If she hasn't directly addressed these patterns with her husband, *and she can safely do so*, Pastor Don will ask if she believes that she can bring these sinful behaviors to her husband. Safety concerns could be (but are not limited to) hearing that there is physical danger by threats against her or her children or weapons in the home, or anything else she reports that would make him concerned for her or the children's safety. Once safety has been established, they move on to discuss her options for moving forward.

After Pastor Don and Brittany discuss options with Mary, if she doesn't feel strong enough (mentally, emotionally, or theologically) to meet with her husband, Pastor Don and Brittany, will encourage her to start working with her counselor to gain clarity about her situation. The counselor will help her to gain an understanding of what she has been experiencing, to think about her marriage situation biblically, and to seek the Lord in the timing of the next step. The counselor may use a domestic abuse assessment (like Darby's in appendix A on page 202) or other materials so that Mary becomes confident to move forward in addressing the sin patterns she has witnessed in her husband.

If Mary addresses the issues with her husband and he "listens," they can reach out to Pastor Don and Brittany, who will help them create a care plan going forward. If he "refuses to listen," then she can ask that Pastor Don and her witnesses meet with her husband to confront him about his sin patterns. (If she doesn't have witnesses, Pastor Don and Brittany may serve in that role.) The meeting can be called by Mary (on her own or with her small group leaders' help), or she can ask her husband to call Pastor Don or Pastor Don can call her husband. Often husbands will make the call because they want an opportunity to be heard—which is what the pastor wants to give him.

In that meeting, Pastor Don will again go over Matthew 18, reading it and then explaining it to Mary's husband, Laurence. Pastor Don, making sure that Laurence has a clear understanding of the Scripture and what is happening, then lays out the agenda for the meeting. This is a general overview of the process:

- Mary will communicate her concerns to Laurence, giving examples of each concern.
- Laurence will be given the opportunity to respond.
    - If he *listens* to Mary, meaning, if he *agrees* with what she has charged, then next steps will be given, including counseling referrals, and a care plan for each spouse individually and for the marriage and family.
    - If he *refuses to listen*—he *disagrees*—then there will be a period of "establishing the charges." This, too, will be clearly explained, with a well-articulated care plan going forward for Mary and for Laurence. As part of this care plan, two witnesses will be identified to walk through the plan with the couple. The plan will include concrete goals that help the witnesses establish the charges, evidence repentance, or show that the charges were false.
- A next meeting will be set for the purpose of discerning whether or not the charges and/or repentance have been established to the satisfaction of Mary and her witnesses. (If Laurence seems to make progress by making good use of counseling and other help, then there most likely will be more than one meeting throughout the discernment process.)

- If he refuses to listen to charges of abuse, Pastor Don will take it to the elder council for next steps.
- If he listens and demonstrates fruit—that is, action—in keeping with repentance (sustained over an appropriate measure of time, to be determined by Pastor Don and other involved elders, with input from Mary and the rest of the team), then they can move toward restoration. See chapter 10 for help in discerning true repentance.

Remember: we establish safety before anything else. The process must be well-defined, clearly articulated, and understood. Written and signed agreements are helpful to assure accountability and lessen misunderstandings. Each person is committed to the process. Everyone understands their roles.

Questions to consider and ask throughout the care process

Throughout the process, we need to thoughtfully consider whether our ministry can be improved. The following questions can help you with that assessment:

- Ask those receiving care how you are doing. Do they feel heard (not necessarily agreed with, but heard)? Are you respecting their autonomy in relation to any church membership agreements? Do they speak up when they have concerns?
- How is everyone on the team doing? How are they being cared for?
- Is each person able to express their thoughts, observations, and opinions? Have you created the space for continued conversation and sharpening one another?

Questions to ask at the end of the process

It's important to assess the ministry throughout the process and at the end. We all are sinners and fall short of the glory of God, but we do want to glorify God in and through our domestic abuse ministry. Wisdom dictates and humility requires that we ask questions of ourselves so that we can grow. "But the wisdom from above is first pure, then peaceable, gentle, open to reason, full of mercy and good fruits, impartial and sincere. And a harvest of righteousness is sown in peace by those who make peace" (James 3:17–18). Humility always wins the day. As you assess the finished process, here are some things to consider:

- How did we first hear about this case? What was the avenue for coming forward?
- Were we biblically faithful? Did we speak the truth in love?
- What was our response?
    - Was it timely? Compassionate? Helpful? Supportive? Confidential?
    - Was safety assessed and/or established at the outset?
    - Were appropriate authorities notified?
    - Was there comprehensive collaboration with other pastors/elders/professionals?
    - Was an effective safety plan created and continually evaluated?
- How were things followed up? Was the follow-up
    - Timely?
    - Supportive?
- Was follow-up initiated by the church—or was communication inadequate?
- Were resources and referrals provided (food, counsel, small groups, Bible studies, etc.)?
- Was appropriate connection to the larger church body facilitated?
- Was a plan made for the abuser to be confronted, discipled, and if necessary, disciplined?
- Was there continued support and/or shepherding of the abused (elder oversight, and/or church body mobilized)?
- What was the resolution?

- Was the abuse resolved (in the marriage and in the church relationship)? Is there a plan for follow-up care and regular check-ins over the next couple of years?
- Are there any loose ends?
- What were the strengths of how we moved with the reporting woman? The alleged abuser?
- What were the weaknesses of how we moved with the reporting woman? The alleged abuser?
- Where do we go from here?

At the beginning of this chapter, I stated that domestic abuse ministry (like every other ministry in the church) is a way to become more and more like our beautiful Savior. My hope in these basic ideas that I've given you to think about is that you will shepherd and counsel people with wisdom, truth, and love. There is not a one-size-fits-all domestic abuse ministry any more than there is for ministry to widows or children or chronically ill or the dying. We love the people before us, and for that, we need Jesus desperately.

> Redeem me from man's oppression,
>   that I may keep your precepts. . . .
> I rise before dawn and cry for help;
>   I hope in your words.
> My eyes are awake before the watches of the night,
>   that I may meditate on your promise.
> Hear my voice according to your steadfast love;
>   O LORD, according to your justice give me life.
>   (Psalm 119:134, 147–49)

> And the people believed; and when they heard that the LORD had visited the people of Israel and that he had seen their affliction, they bowed their heads and worshiped. (Exodus 4:31)

We address domestic abuse in the church for the same reason we address any other struggle or entrenched sin—to restore worship to God. My prayer is that we all—abused, abuser, elders, counselors, helpers—will worship at the feet of Jesus together. O glorious day!

CHAPTER 3

• • • •

A Team-Based Approach to Domestic Abuse

Darby A. Strickland, Kirsten Christianson, Joy Forrest, Greg Wilson, and Chris Moles

As we have discussed, we are suggesting churches should consider establishing a team-based approach when encountering domestic abuse. This ensures that key members in the church community understand their role in responding to domestic abuse and that they can work together effectively to support survivors and hold perpetrators accountable. By adopting a team-based approach within the church, pastors, church leaders, and lay leaders can collaborate with each other, as well as establish needed relationships with law enforcement, social service providers, and other organizations to create a comprehensive and coordinated response to domestic abuse. This team-based approach can help ensure that survivors receive the necessary support and services and perpetrators are held accountable for their actions.

Sometimes church leadership takes time to build consensus about whether abuse has occurred. These situations are difficult to navigate and can strain unity, especially if the church leadership does not have experience in assessing for coercive control. Having a response team of informed, experienced helpers such as both spouses' counselors, the church crisis person, and a victim advocate weigh in on the presence and severity of abuse in each case blesses the church leadership as they seek to make ecclesiastical decisions and provide care. Our hope is that the following case study of initial responses will present at least a glimpse through the lens of different care team members, showing how different perspectives can reveal or address blind spots and improve care. Care team members include the following:

- **Victim's counselor**: Comes alongside the victim to help her recognize and respond to the patterns of abuse her spouse has subjected her to. She helps connect the sufferer to wise resources, but most importantly to God's Word and his heart for her.
- **Church crisis care coordinator**: Works directly with those in crisis situations at the church to provide care under the oversight of the supervising pastor and in partnership with assigned elders. In situations for which care teams are necessary, she facilitates communication between team members, as well as providing counsel and assistance as necessary.
- **Victim advocate**: Works directly with the victim to help them navigate the complex issues they face through support and resources. Advocates may also operate to help churches, counselors, and others involved understand victim's concerns and more effectively support the survivors and their children.
- **Perpetrator counselor**: Helps guide the perpetrator toward the goal of seeing, owning, hating, and turning from his abusive behavior. This counselor should also be able to assess the perpetrator's corrupted perceptions that lead to his corrupted behaviors. If this counselor doesn't have training in psychological assessment, he should be able to refer his counselee to an appropriate clinician capable of conducting such an assessment.
- **Pastor** or a member of the church's pastoral team: Oversees the care process from the church perspective and partners with the team to inform leadership of progress or setbacks and

provide guidance to the team regarding theological concerns, policies, and procedures regarding care and church discipline.

Although each person takes on a different role, you will notice that there is some overlap, especially when it comes to the victim's safety. Not only is safety a key priority, it is best established when everyone on the team works together to achieve it. Another area of shared territory will be establishing the patterns of abuse. It is wise to have many people establishing and documenting the abuse. This is important because it is wise to verify the presence and the severity of abuse. Also, sometimes it takes time for a victim to divulge and organize their story so we work as a team to gather data. What is uncovered will also inform safety concerns. Our hope is to give you a vision of how you can coordinate ministering well to both spouses ensnared by the dynamics of domestic abuse. Let's look at an example of how a team-based approach could work within a specific case.

Jane and Jim

Jane is a young, twenty-six-year-old wife with one toddler. She has been married two years to Jim, a twenty-eight-year-old airline pilot. They are both active church members and well-respected in the community. Jane reached out to her church for help after a crisis point. She was prompted to call for help because one day after working extensively in their vegetable garden, she had gotten behind in tending to the housework. After cleaning the kitchen, she went back outside to water what she had just planted and found that most of her plants had been pulled up. All the flowers had their blooms cut off. She was distraught. Jim admitted that he did it in retaliation for the chaos in the house. He yelled, "You don't have time to keep a garden, just look at the mess inside!" After a thirty-minute obscenity-laced vile lecture that transpired in front of their child, Jane called some friends to pick her up, and she is currently staying with them.

Previously Jane saw a biblical counselor for panic attacks and during these sessions, some abusive dynamics in her marriage were uncovered. But this last event led Jane to see the seriousness of Jim's behaviors, and both she and her counselor thought it wise to bring in other supports. Jane then made the decision to contact her church for help.

When the church crisis care coordinator spoke with her, Jane revealed that she was afraid of her husband and stated, "I can't take it anymore." He worked a job that took him away for days at a time, and then he was home for several days. When he was gone, there was peace and she could breathe. When he was home, she had to be very careful about what she said. But lately she said things had gotten even worse.

To better understand some of the basic history, the crisis care coordinator had an intake conversation with Jane. She discovered that Jim was often irritable, sarcastic, and very critical, even in front of their son. At times, he would fly into a rage at the drop of a hat. He called her names (the b-word, contrarian, a bad mother, a weak woman, etc.). Jim accused her of being too independent, unsubmissive, and stubborn. He also said, "A godly woman knows how important it is to take care of her man."

When asked, Jane said that Jim had never hit her, but he had grabbed her and thrown things at her. She reported he had never physically harmed their son. Jane reported that this was not the first time she had asked for help. They had talked to another couple about their struggles and had tried other marriage counselors, but nothing had seemed to work. In fact, things had gotten worse.

Counselor Working with the Victim: Darby A. Strickland

My initial goals for counseling victims of domestic abuse typically include these six elements:

1. Perform initial intake process with a safety assessment.
2. Help the victim navigate wise and godly ways of responding to the abuse.

3. Coordinate care with the care team if it is allowed. To speak with other members of the team the victim would need to sign a release of information granting permission to do so. However, we would also have to determine which pieces of information it was safe to share.
4. Provide support for the victim and help them cope, process, and eventually heal from the trauma of abuse.
5. Work toward restoring the victim's identity in Christ.
6. When invited by the victim, participate in coordinated care that involves issues like potential separation or reconciliation (if sustained repentance is established).

I had been counseling Jane for about three months before she called her church for help. She came in for counseling because she was stressed to the point of having panic attacks a few times a week. She revealed that she felt like she was failing as a mother. After asking why she thought so, Jane shared the ways in which her husband disparaged her parenting. When I learned how Jim was ridiculing, lecturing, and humiliating her, I did a basic abuse screening (see appendix A) and a safety assessment and plan (see appendix B).

Initially, Jane was conflicted. She vacillated, thinking that she was the problem and was overreacting to saying that she feared Jim when he was angry. She just wanted to know what to do to keep Jim from being angry. After probing her for stories of times when Jim was cruel and punishing, I began to educate her on pernicious patterns of entitlement that lead a person to be controlling. As Jane gained categories for the types of punishments and behaviors that she was enduring, she began to see worrisome patterns in Jim's treatment of her. We discussed the various ways that she responded to Jim's harsh treatment of her and how she attempted to protect their child from his anger. My screening for potential child abuse thankfully did not show that Jim had harmed their child.

Over time, Jane saw that no matter how well she responded to Jim's demands for an incredibly clean home, intimacy, and not bothering him with requests for help or money, he was rarely satisfied and often angry. In fact, he typically found something to criticize her for and often lectured her or threw things at her when frustrated. It became clear that her panic attacks were tied to living under constant stress.

We began thinking about who in her church she might appeal to for help and support. While Jane would be served well by caring friends who could pray for and support her, with the level of intensity unfolding at home, it was clear that she had a higher level of need and was ready to have others step in and help. Jane wanted someone to care for Jim; she loved him and wanted him to see the ways he was being destructive and repent of them so they could stay a family. We decided that she should reach out and see if her church had anything in place to help a marriage in crisis. Thankfully, Jane's church had someone who served as a point person, and Jane prayed about the courage to ask for help.

After the garden incident, it became clear that Jim's behavior was escalating so Jane needed to enact the safety plan that we had worked on. She took her toddler to the location she had designated and called the church crisis person for help. Jane felt that it was an answer to prayer, as it helped her move forward in getting more help. Jane had provided me with a release of information so I was able to speak with the church leaders and express my concerns. I was thankful to learn the church was willing to prioritize her safety and connect her to an advocate.

As I continue to counsel Jane, I will be looking to coordinate care with others on the team and again screen for safety as confrontations start with Jim. My main role will be to help Jane navigate the many decisions she will face in the months ahead. For her to do that with confidence, I will spend a considerable amount of time helping her discover in Scripture how God wants her to respond when someone has grievously sinned against her. This will take a tremendous amount of prayer and discernment. She will wonder what repentance looks like and whether she is wrong to separate while she is waiting for it.

We will continue to address her anxiety and encourage her to cry out to a God who rescues the oppressed. Jim used many cruel words and left Jane full of shame and fear, so I will want her to know how much love her heavenly Father has for her. I will help her see that Jesus also knows what it is like to be shamed and rejected, and that he promises to be with her throughout her journey—no matter where it goes.

Church Crisis Care Coordinator: Kirsten Christianson

As the church's designated crisis care coordinator, working with and/or at the direction of the pastor, our goals when contacted about a potential domestic abuse situation include the following, assuming that both the wife *and* the husband regularly attend or are members of the church:

1. Meet, hear, and care for the church member who has been referred. Ascertain what type of help she is looking for from the church, and what her hoped-for outcome is.
2. Assess what resources will be needed depending on the level of brokenness. Sample questions would be the following: Has she had to flee her home? Does she have access to funds? Does she have relational support?
3. Explain the care process to her. It is important to do this carefully. It is best if she has someone with her to process. Often when a marriage has reached the point at which a spouse has either had to flee or reach out to pastors, it is emotionally overwhelming, scary, and can create barriers to productive communication. If possible, introduce the care team to her, including the roles and responsibilities of each person. (Depending on your church size, etc., not all of these roles may be separate.) What can she expect from the church? Does she want the pastors to reach out to her husband? Is she ready for that step or does she need more counseling time? Determine if she is in agreement with the process, answering

any questions. Offer time for prayer and counsel for her to consider what she wants to do.

4. Once the process begins, and each of them have agreed to the process, we create a care plan for her/them. This requires input from the pastor, counselors, advocate, and discipler. This care plan is living and dynamic; as counseling progresses, there will be changes and updates. Revising and updating the care plan each month is wise.
5. Present a care plan to each of them, individually. Again, make sure that they understand the process, the goals and desires, and what care and accountability looks like.
6. Refer each spouse to an individual counselor (if they don't already have one), as well as an advocate/discipler for her and a discipler/mentor for him (both of these people should have had abuse training).
7. Coordinate care and accountability, facilitating team communication and information-sharing, and ensuring timely follow-up.
8. Update the pastor as needed on progress, as well as if something needs his attention. *If discipline is going to be on the table at any point, this must be communicated to the husband and the wife.* It is important that the offender should understand when the discipline process will start and what that will look like.

Note: Churches have their own structures. I will be responding from one possible structure; it matters less what the structure is than that there is an identified structure by which people know how to get help when their marriages are imploding.

Prior to our meeting with Jane, Pastor Chris and I made ourselves familiar with the information that the counselor had passed along. We then invited Jane to bring a supportive friend, someone she trusted and who would give her wise counsel. In our meeting, we assessed her safety, even though the counselor had already done so. We want to make sure that nothing has changed since the last assessment. In addition, in the time between the counselor's assessment and when we meet, other things may have occurred that need attention. We confirmed that she had access to finances and that no threat had been made to move or withhold money or payment of regular bills. We asked questions such as these (please see Short Safety Form in appendix B):

- Are there weapons in the home?
- Have there been threats to harm her, the children, others, or himself?
- Is she safe with her friends?
- Are there children, and what help do they need?

After we assessed Jane's safety and helped her make a safety plan, we proceeded to go over the assessment Jane's counselor had shared with us, and we asked any follow-up questions to gain a clear picture of what her marriage and parenting life had been like in the home. Additionally, we sought to glean any additional stories or information that may have risen to the surface between the time she had met with her counselor and when she met with us.

We also took the time to hear her concerns about reaching out to the church for help. What worried her? What were her felt needs? Were there any relationships (small group, Bible study, etc.) that she would like help managing as she and her husband receive help from the church? How were they involved in the church, and did she or he need to step away for a season to attend to the family? (This is not a given; wisdom and discernment are needed to see what is best for each of them.)

Throughout the meeting, we paid attention to Jane's fears and tried to encourage her faith in the Lord. Like most believing women, Jane didn't want to displease the Lord, nor did she wish to "throw her husband under the bus." She reiterated, "I am not perfect. I have sins that I struggle with too. I just don't know what to do; I want our marriage to look like the marriages of others in the church and

Bible study. I don't want to feel crushed all the time. I don't want to be afraid anymore." We reassured her that we didn't assume that she was perfect, and that the Lord does have sanctification for her too. We assured her that it was good and wise for her to reach out for help after the years she had spent suggesting and then imploring her husband to come with her to talk to a pastor. Jane responded, "Please, I just want help for us!"

We excused ourselves to pray and talk through what we believed would be wise next steps. Then we stepped back into the room and offered Jane some options: Did she want the church to reach out to Jim? Did she think that she needed to continue her own counseling to better understand her situation before the pastors reached out to her husband? Jane very much wanted Pastor Chris to meet with Jim. She had texted Jim to tell him that she was talking to Pastor Chris and that the pastor wants to talk to him too. Jane stated that Jim was waiting for the pastor's call. We prayed with Jane and her friend, and they headed back to her friend's house. The pastor and I prayerfully strategized our next steps (Proverbs 11:14).

In this situation, *given we had Jane's permission and input into how to best proceed*, Pastor Chris decided to reach out to her husband and invite him in for a conversation with the two of us. Jim came in the next day. (*Note*: when meeting with the offender, we do not reveal to him what his wife shared about him and their marriage. We do use that information to help us ask good questions so that we can hear more about incidents and gauge how he reports the same incidents.)

During that conversation, we learned more of his thoughts and experiences of the marriage, listening to how he reported events in his marriage. We heard his struggles, and we asked questions to better understand how he thought about marriage, about being a husband and father, and about leading his family in love. Jim admitted that he "gets out of hand sometimes," but says, "She provokes me. She doesn't just listen to what I say and decide. I come home, and the place is messy—toys everywhere, and she isn't happy to see me." Jim shared that he wants to make his marriage with Jane work, and that he does want to grow, but that she has to become a meeker wife. "When I want her thoughts, I will ask for them."

We asked Jim if he was willing to do some individual counseling. At first, he balked at trying something other than marriage counseling. When it was pointed out that they had tried that several times before, he reluctantly agreed to give it a go. We explained to him that we were concerned at the destructive behaviors we were hearing, and we believed that counseling would help him examine his heart and address the concerning pattern of behavior. In addition, we let him know that we were pairing him with a discipler, someone who could be in the Word with him, perhaps attend some counseling sessions with him, and help him make the best use of what he was learning in counseling and the Word. He was amenable to this as well. We thanked him, and then gave him a few counseling referrals, asking him to let us know when he had secured a counselor and an ROI so that his counselor would be able to talk with us. (*Note*: when Pastor Chris receives the signed ROI, this confirms that Jim is going to follow through with the process.)

At this point, we have not used the word *abuse*, for several reasons. First, in my experience, most women are not usually ready or wanting the word to be used. They want behaviors to be named and stopped because the vast majority of women want their marriages to succeed. We want to go at her pace. Second, we want to give him the opportunity to work with a counselor and walk him toward understanding how he is treating his wife and what he thinks would describe the behavior. For instance, Greg Wilson doesn't go right to that word *abuse*, but rather he helps the husband name the behaviors he is inflicting on his wife and children so that the husband can own it for himself.

After Jim had done what we had asked and the proper ROIs were in place, we then secured an advocate for Jane and a discipler for Jim and made the appropriate introductions.

Once the counselors and other care team members had some time to settle in, I reached out to the counselors to help us formulate a care plan for the husband and the wife. This plan would be specific to their situation. It would have concrete, measurable goals for each of them, and also may include other elements for which they need guidance (for example: how to manage finances, communication guidelines, parenting time for the children, communication guidelines for them, etc.), as well as clearly articulated expectations for the care team.

From that point on, there will be regular check-ins for the team to share information, discern progress, and plan next steps. My role as the crisis care person at the church will vary, depending on how the situation continues to unfold. With Pastor Chris's input and direction, I will establish that either progress is or isn't happening, that information is flowing well between the team (so that people are not giving counsel in a vacuum), and that Pastor Chris is regularly updated so that he can shepherd the couple.

Victim's Advocate: Joy Forrest

Goals of a victim's advocate are primarily focused on meeting the wide variety of needs of victims of domestic abuse. Some standard goals include the following:

1. Meet for initial interview to identify abusive patterns, safety issues, and practical needs.
2. Encourage and assist her with documenting the abuse.
3. Help her explore options and connect her with resources.
4. Meet regularly to assess current needs, risks, and concerns, and to explore possible solutions.
5. Encourage her to make her own decisions.
6. Keep care team updated on needs, risks, and concerns (this will include her assessment of the abuser's progress).

As an advocate for survivors of domestic abuse, I was glad to assist when Kirsten called me. I understood that Jane would likely be sharing her private and traumatic experiences multiple times to multiple people, which could be overwhelming and difficult for her. My goal was to assist the team by serving as a resource and support for Jane.

I am grateful that Kïrsten took the time to inform Jane about the benefits of having an advocate and asked her permission to bring one in. Our initial meeting was not only designed to introduce Jane and myself but also to get an overall picture of the problem and to assess safety issues. I worked closely with Kïrsten, listening and asking clarifying questions to determine abusive patterns and safety.

These first meetings require a great deal of unity and cooperation between Kïrsten as the care team coordinator and me as the advocate. I stay in close contact with Jane and regularly relay her concerns and wishes to other team members through updates to Kïrsten and during team meetings. My role will continue to be representing Jane's perspective and ensuring that her needs are clearly communicated to the team. Because of the nature of the role, I am usually the first to hear of new developments, threats, and needs and to alert the team promptly. This is just one of many benefits of having an advocate on the team.

Another benefit of having an advocate is to help the team get a clearer understanding of what is truly happening in Jane's marriage. Her reports, like many provided by victims of abuse, can often be fragmented and confusing. My role saves the team time and energy by sorting through her scattered reports of abuse and helping create a more precise assessment of her major concerns. Therefore, I helped create a timeline and document the abuse, which was vitally important to successful intervention. I also provided referrals to local and national resources to help her move forward—support groups, bill assistance agencies, domestic violence attorneys and counselors, and resources for her children.

As always, safety is our top priority. Even though Jane had not yet reported any physical harm at the hands of her husband, the potential for escalation was significant. Jim had already engaged in destroying something she valued, showing that he was willing to use destructive force to get his way. During my initial visits with Jane, I assessed the increased risk of danger and potential future lethality. As a result, I also connected her with a local domestic violence agency for consultation regarding a possible protective order. These agencies may be able to reduce the stress of filing for the order by allowing her to make the request to a judge via closed-circuit television and thereby avoid a trip to the courthouse. These agencies also have a wealth of information on obtaining housing as well as legal and financial assistance.

Domestic abuse cases are complex, time-consuming, and often continue for years. There are many possible outcomes, and the marriage may or may not survive. However, my goal is to support Jane through whatever comes her way, to help her overcome barriers, regain agency, and find the best path forward. I look forward to continuing to serve Jane and partner with Kïrsten and the team.

Counselor Working with the Perpetrator: Greg Wilson

As the counselor working with the perpetrator of domestic abuse, in addition to seeking to maximize the victim's safety, my goals are focused on identifying the specific issues at work in this particular person and helping him grow and change. While I, Greg, am a professional, licensed counselor, I recognize that many reading this book may be biblical counselors or church leaders.

Depending on where you live and what local resources are, each reader will have to make the best determination about who can best counsel the perpetrator. Either way, this person must be someone with training and experience in the dynamics of domestic abuse and in best practices for perpetrator intervention. If there is not such a person in your local area (or if you do not know them), you should never skimp on training and experience in domestic abuse and perpetrator intervention. There are Batterer Intervention and Prevention Programs (BIPP) in almost every local area. I would advise anyone who may end up working with this population to acquaint themselves with such local programs and domestic abuse agencies prior to engaging in this work. There is no substitute for training and experience. And without it, you can do a great deal of damage. Group programs like BIPP or the Men of Peace (MOP) program that Chris Moles and I have developed can be very beneficial, even in conjunction with individual counseling. So if you don't have someone like me in your local area, a BIPP program with trained interventionists can be a very helpful adjunct to your work. Even a secular BIPP program can be a helpful partner as you bring the gospel to bear in your counseling.

As a counselor for the perpetrator, I work with him to

1. Conduct an initial intake process, including a risk assessment.
2. Develop a treatment plan.
3. Work with the rest of the care team if allowed via ROI.
4. Either provide or refer for treatment for any underlying issues: trauma, mental health diagnoses, physical challenges, etc.
5. Labor to help him see, own, hate, and turn from his sin; the goal is true repentance.
6. Participate, as asked or if necessary, in whatever reconciliation counseling might follow repentance.

As a mental health provider, I believe it is important to begin any counseling relationship with a standard initial intake interview, regardless of the referral source. When Jim was referred to me through the church-based team, I asked him why he sought counseling, how things were going in his marriage and other relationships, and I attempted to gather a complete history, including prior experiences with counseling and mental health. I also asked him what he hoped to accomplish through counseling.

While Jim initially attempted to frame our time together as marriage counseling via proxy, after significant back and forth, we agreed that his marriage was suffering in large part due to choices that he had made, many of which were destructive. Moving forward, my goal was to help Jim name his destructive behaviors and grow in awareness about how they negatively impacted his relationship.

Although Jane or Kirsten may not mention the word *abuse* out of fear of potential retaliatory responses, I always assess for risk and ensure that Jane's safety is always on our radar. It is tempting to believe that separation will end the abusive behavior, but an abuser intent on causing harm will try to track their spouse down wherever they are. Post-separation abuse is a common occurrence, and it is important to recognize that potential.

After the initial intake interview, Jim agreed to continue seeing me, and we developed his treatment plan collaboratively. This included counseling goals to work on addressing his corrupt perceptions and behaviors, any mental health diagnoses he was presenting, and strategies to help him see his sin, own it, hate it, and begin to turn from it. If I was not trained to make the appropriate mental health assessment, I would have referred Jim to a clinical psychologist or other clinician who was trained to do so.

I recommended that Jim enroll in the church's MOP program in addition to individual counseling. Recovery from abusive behaviors is a long-term process that requires significant commitment, and I believed that engaging in a robust recovery program would give Jim the best chance for change. Informed consent is an important aspect of good treatment, and it is critical that Jim knew up front what he was getting into and what he was agreeing to.

Thankfully, Jim agreed to allow me to collaborate with other members of the treatment team by signing a release of information for each team member. Even if Jim chose not to agree to informed consent our work would continue along the parallel tracks of addressing Jim's individual issues and working on repenting from and making amends for his abusive behaviors. The victim's safety would remain foremost in my mind, and while collaboration with the team is always ideal, the real test of Jim's repentance and growth would be observed by the victim and the shepherding team. Regardless of whether he agreed to collaborate, my obligation was to provide care when I had the expertise to do so, or refer him to someone who did.

Although the ideal goal was for Jim to find healing for his issues, repent of his abuse, be reconciled to God, and, if possible, be reconciled to Jane and his son, the sad truth is that in most cases, this does not happen. My hope for Jim was that he would become a more peaceful man and be reconciled to God. In many cases, the best perpetrator work has been done after consequences are experienced. Sometimes a person has to lose everything to gain what is most important.

Pastor: Reverend Chris Moles

As Jim and Jane's pastor, my goals are focused on providing spiritual oversight and ensuring each person has what they need to grow and flourish:

1. Listen to disclosures with compassion and care. Lead by listening well and documenting.
2. Prayer is the first work. Bathe the situation in prayer and commit to a posture of prayerful dependence.
3. Know and follow local reporting laws and connect with service providers that best fill the needed roles to offer comfort and care.
4. Be prepared to thoughtfully answer questions regarding the church's theology, polity, and procedures in cases of abuse.
5. Offer to assist in any way possible, such as providing common meeting space, benevolence resources, deacon care, etc.

As a pastor, I understand that being among the first people a victim of abuse will disclose to is a tremendous responsibility. Jane's willingness to include me in the team learning about her situation with Jim warrants the discipline to listen carefully to her story. I know that it can be tempting to jump in with opinions and procedures, but I believe it is important to gather all the relevant information and assess the situation before making any decisions. This is especially true considering that Jane has separated from Jim. The temptation to question further regarding the state of the marriage is real for me as a pastor, as I have been more thoroughly trained in marriage-based care, and my church places a high value on marriage. I want to lean heavily on the team's wisdom and Kïrsten's leadership to guard myself from rushing ahead by promoting my own priorities or even the church's comfort over the needed care for Jane.

In addition to listening, I would reaffirm my commitment to prayerful dependence on the Holy Spirit and a commitment to God's Word. I believe that prayer is the first and most significant work to do.

Second, I want to make sure Kïrsten and the team has everything they need in order to successfully offer church-based resources for care and answer questions regarding theology, church policy, and procedures, and, of course, coordinating team efforts through the church calendar and facilities. I want to not only serve Jane and Jim through this process but the team as well, so Kïrsten and I are already scheduling regular calls for updates and team meetings for clarity and resourcing. I already anticipate that there will be points in the process in which I am asked to lead, but I want to set the tone for the team-based response by taking the posture of a servant in these early stages. When the team is ready to move forward with an intervention, in particular if Jim allows Greg (the perpetrator's counselor) to collaborate with the team, I or one of our pastors will be available to follow up with Jim on homework and growth plans and offer to walk with him through the MOP or attend a local BIPP group with him.

I understand that assisting the team to provide for Jane's safety and John's repentance will require a great deal of time and energy. While I may eventually be taking the lead on finalizing church discipline or long-term discipleship, I believe it is important to learn from and defer to a trained, qualified team of experts in these initial stages of care. Working with a team will allow me to learn key truths that are central to Jim and Jane's spiritual needs and plans for growth. Engaging in the recommendations of the team can help form short-term expectations and long-term discipleship priorities as the case develops.

Our hope is that you too will agree that caring for a victim of domestic violence is best done with a team-based approach. Having a comprehensive and collaborative approach that is meant to address domestic violence in an effective and coordinated way has been used in a secular environment for decades. The commonly implemented community-coordinated response (CCR) is a collaborative approach that recognizes the complexity of domestic violence and the need for a coordinated effort to address it. This approach invites various stakeholders—law enforcement agencies, social service providers, healthcare professionals, advocates, and community leaders—to the table for identifying, responding to, and preventing domestic abuse.

By adopting a similar approach, churches can encourage communication and cooperation among all parties involved. The team-based approach aims to help survivors of domestic abuse get the support and services they need, while holding perpetrators accountable for their actions. Within our church communities, adopting a team-based approach based on the CCR model can be especially helpful for ensuring that everyone understands their role in responding to domestic abuse and that they can work together effectively to provide support to survivors. By following this model, churches can create a safer environment for survivors of domestic abuse within their community and help to prevent domestic violence from happening in the future.

CHAPTER 4

....

First Things First: Listening Well to Domestic Abuse Survivors

Joy Forrest

Domestic abuse (DA) is likely the most complex and difficult problem most counselors will ever face. Perhaps one reason for this is that these issues can be extremely counterintuitive. Abusive people are often charming, confident, and convincing, while their victims can present as unstable, angry, and confused. In over two decades of working with women who have experienced DA, I have found that very few of them come to counseling with an understanding that what they are experiencing is actually abuse. More often, they show up for counseling to get help for their marriages—they want help with improving communication, becoming better wives, or ways to help their husbands express their anger in healthier ways. Abuse is rarely mentioned.

If those experiencing abuse have difficulty identifying it, it can be even more perplexing to counselors who get only small glimpses of the problem through interviews with guarded counselees. Victims of abuse often fail to disclose the abuse for fear of how their husbands may react, especially in marriage counseling sessions where their abusers are present. It is generally wise to separate couples and move to individual counseling any time abuse is suspected. To effectively counsel victims of domestic abuse, the counselor must consider some of the characteristics of domestic abuse survivors and carefully provide what they most need.

Characteristics of Domestic Abuse Survivors

In order to provide helpful counsel to survivors of domestic abuse, it is crucial that counselors first become proficient in understanding the dynamics of coercive control and its impacts on victims. Let's look at the effects of such abuse.

Survivors of domestic abuse have been traumatized.

Survivors need you to understand the impacts of what they and their children have experienced, even if there has been no physical injury. The overwhelming majority of domestic abuse survivors (80 percent or more),[1] along with their children, exhibit all the signs of post-traumatic stress. Situations of extreme oppression without physical injury often lead to stress-related medical issues, such as autoimmune disorders, high blood pressure, gastric maladies, migraine headaches, and more. Traumatized people often present as irritable, angry, scattered, anxiety-ridden, and unstable. In addition, those who experience *ongoing* complex trauma often exhibit "feelings of hopelessness, and even loss of their basic beliefs about the meaning of life, including their faith in God."[2] They are highly reactive and easily triggered. These responses are somatic because trauma is held in the body and impacts the entire person (Job 3:24–26; Psalm 55:5). Counsel that fails to consider the physical impacts of abuse further traumatizes victims and burdens them with unrealistic expectations of their ability to heal and move forward in a timely manner. You can read more about the characteristics and impact of trauma in Chapter 6.

---

1. Edward S. Kubany, Mari A. McCaig, and Janet Laconsay, *Healing the Trauma of Domestic Violence: A Workbook for Women* (Oakland, CA: New Harbinger Publications, 2004), 15.

2. Judith Herman, *Trauma and Recovery: The Aftermath of Violence—From Domestic Abuse to Political Terror* (New York: Basic Books, 1997), 121–22.

Survivors of domestic abuse have a warped view of God and feel disconnected from him.

A woman victimized by her husband may think that God is angry with her because she hasn't been able to save the marriage. She may see God as detached and indifferent, or she may even be angry with him because she has done her best to be a good wife, yet things have only gotten worse. Her abuser may have used Scripture to justify his sense of entitlement, so she may perceive God as a harsh authoritarian who sides with the abuser. Initially focusing on her sin will likely serve to broaden the chasm between her and God. She needs counsel that reconnects her to the goodness of God.[3] Once she is restored to him, he will gently help her see where she needs to repent. Generally speaking, the victim's sin is the opposite of what most counselors believe. It is not that she provoked her husband to abuse her; rather, it is that she made her marriage an idol and her abuser bigger than God. A careful reorientation toward God and his ways will help change that perspective.

Survivors of domestic abuse have a warped view of self.

Women in abusive homes carry a great deal of shame. They wonder what they did to deserve such harsh treatment. They may even believe it is God's judgment for past sin. They don't understand the lavish grace he has for them, and they have no concept of their identity in Christ. Good counsel will help them understand their value and let them know that they are "accepted in the beloved" (Ephesians 1:6 KJV).

Survivors of domestic abuse take responsibility and blame for the problems in their marriages.

A wife living in an oppressive marriage is intimately aware of her faults. Encouraging her to confess her sin to her abuser may seem

---

3. Joy Forrest, *Called to Peace: A Survivor's Guide to Finding Peace & Healing After Domestic Abuse* (Raleigh, NC: Blue Ink, 2018); Joy Forrest, "Lesson 5: Knowing God" in the *Called to Peace Companion Workbook* (Raleigh, NC: Blue Ink, 2019), 34–43. These resources give an extensive list of Scriptures in a Scripture database that can be used to help victims of abuse correct misperceptions about God.

like the wise, Christian thing to do, but this actually gives her husband ammunition to further the abuse.[4] Counsel that encourages her to focus on her shortcomings, rather than deal with the oppression, increases her sense of shame and hopelessness. It will simply reinforce what her abuser is already telling her—that everything is her fault. We counsel those who are oppressed that "A bruised reed he will not break, and a smoldering wick he will not snuff out. In faithfulness he will bring forth justice . . ." (Isaiah 42:3 NIV).

Survivors of domestic abuse feel more like hostages than wives.

When I teach about domestic abuse, I often describe it as domestic terrorism. Abusive husbands lord it over their wives, instill great fear, and create uncertainty about when the next attack will come. It's completely unpredictable. Some inconsequential thing that never bothered the husband before might suddenly set off a new tidal wave of fury. The wife and the children live with a constant sense of impending doom, but they often fail to recognize how his harsh control has impacted them. His outbursts may not happen constantly; rather, they are often interspersed with periods of favor that can last for weeks or even months at a time. During these pleasant times, women and children let down their guard. Inevitably the abuse returns. These periods of favor keep victims confused. Often abused wives do not define their husband's actions as abusive. They will more likely express confusion about the problems in their marriage.

What Domestic Abuse Survivors Most Need from You

How can a counselor best aid an abuse survivor? Let's look at several specific things you can do to make this time easier for her.

4. Joy Forrest, "Don't Confess Your Sins to an Abuser!" *Joyful Surrender*, blog, February 9, 2018, https://joyforrest.wordpress.com/2018/02/09/dont-confess-your-sins-to-an-abuser/.

Domestic abuse survivors need you to keep their disclosure of abuse confidential until they are ready to confront their husbands' sin.

If a woman discloses abuse to you and you automatically confront her abuser, you will undoubtedly put her at risk of greater harm. Safety must be paramount in these situations, so consulting with a domestic violence expert to make a safety plan with the abused woman is crucial.[5] Wise counselors will also avoid sharing her report with others without the wife's permission. Many women have reported that when their pastors/counselors shared their predicament with the church staff, news spread quickly within the church and put them at risk. Every effort must be made to safeguard this information until a safety plan has been made and until she feels ready. This could take months—or even years.

Domestic abuse survivors should determine the pace for potential reconciliation.

Many women are condemned for their unwillingness to go back to someone who has never truly repented or proven to be trustworthy. Many times these women separate and reconcile multiple times, only to find the abuse worsens after each reconciliation. Often their husbands *appear* repentant, but after reuniting, it becomes obvious there was no genuine change. Wise counselors must recognize the propensity of abusers to feign genuine repentance and respect the woman's hesitation to reconcile based on promising words and a few months of changed behavior. In our work with victims, we allow the wife to make the call on whether or not her husband is truly repentant and whether or not to move forward with reconciliation. *The well-being of the victim and her children should be the primary goal of counseling, rather than saving the marriage.*

---

5. The National Domestic Violence Hotline (1-800-799-7233; thehotline.org) can help connect you with a local advocate who can help with safety planning, and Called to Peace Ministries may be able to connect you with a faith-based advocate (calledtopeace.org).

Domestic abuse survivors need your help to obtain safety.

Even if a harsh, abusive husband has never inflicted physical harm on his wife, she will still endure the severe impacts of trauma, both physically and emotionally. In addition, we know that domestic abuse is typically progressive over time, and without effective intervention, it will most likely worsen. Situations of extreme control may not turn to physical violence until decades later, but they can even end in attempted murder. If the abuse becomes so unbearable that the victim decides to leave, she may find she is in even more danger than if she stayed. Up to 75 percent of all domestic violence homicides happen after the victim leaves.[6] Helpers will need to assist victims by providing for their safety. A well-trained domestic violence advocate can help with safety planning. It is crucial that helpers do not give advice that endangers your counselee. If those who come alongside are unfamiliar with or lack expertise with this issue, it is imperative that they reach out to those with specific training and experience in domestic abuse.

Domestic abuse survivors need to know that they are not responsible for the abuse!

Domestic abuse is always the choice of the abuser, and there's no excuse for it. Victims of abuse may very well seem angry and reactive. This is partially a result of post-traumatic stress and partially from an innate, God-given sense of justice. Abuse is oppression. It is not the result of typical marital conflict in which two parties spur each other on and one spouse loses control. Angry wives are often seen as the problem in the marriage, even when their anger is a reaction to extreme injustice. A few years ago, a pastor told me a story of an abusive situation in which he knew the husband was guilty, "but then he got saved and the wife became the abusive one." In reality, the

6. Jana Kasperkevic, "Private Violence: Up to 75% of Abused Women Who Are Murdered Are Killed after Leaving Their Partners," *The Guardian*, October 20, 2014, https://www.theguardian.com/money/us-money-blog/2014/oct/20/domestic-private-violence-women-men-abuse-hbo-ray-rice.

husband learned to put on a better show and gained the church's support. The wife was so frustrated that her demeanor showed inappropriate, overt anger so she was counseled to forgive and forget. As I sat with this woman trying to determine patterns, I found that her husband was extremely abusive to the children—a situation that would anger most of us. Counselors must recognize that even if a wife is responding sinfully to oppression, the injustice is still the crux of the problem. Wise counsel will first acknowledge the injustice she has experienced and God's hatred of it. After this, she will be more open to receiving instruction on how to respond without sinning.

Note that this counsel will *not* be to simply forgive and forget. I have seen this sort of counsel many times over the years, and it generally makes the victim responsible for the restoration of the family. It also fails to hold the abuser accountable for his sin. According to 2 Corinthians 7:11, godly sorrow in repentance is evidenced by a zeal to make things right. That burden should be on the abuser, not the victim.

Domestic abuse survivors need you to care more for their souls than for their marriages.

Victims of domestic abuse need counsel that reconnects them to God's goodness and his heart for the oppressed. They need their understanding of misused Scriptures corrected.[7] They may actually feel like God cares more for their marriages than for their lives. When counselors focus on the marriage, they simply reinforce the lies they already believe about God and themselves.[8]

---

7. "When Scriptures Are Used to Oppress—Part 1," Called to Peace Ministries, conversations with Chris Moles, Darby Strickland, and Joy Forrest, October 24, 2019, https://vimeo.com/368672088; "When Scriptures Are Used to Oppress—Part 2," Called to Peace Ministries, conversations with Chris Moles, Darby Strickland, and Joy Forrest, October 28, 2019, https://vimeo.com/369453790. These conversations give more information about the Scriptures commonly used to oppress.

8. Joy Forrest, "The Worst Kind of Counselor," blog, Called to Peace Ministries, November 27, 2015, https://www.calledtopeace.org/the-worst-kind-of-counselor/. This gives more information on why this type of counsel is unhelpful.

Setting the Oppressed Free

Understanding these realities about domestic abuse survivors can help you avoid common counseling pitfalls that can inadvertently add to their sense of condemnation. When we fail to respond wisely to this sort of oppression, we can very easily find ourselves reinforcing the abuse, instead of drawing them (and their children) to the lavish love and grace of our Savior.

If you find yourself counseling a victim of domestic abuse,[9] it is important to avoid treating it as a typical case of marital conflict. Instead, seek to reflect God's heart for the oppressed. This involves listening intently to her story and acknowledging the severe injustices she has experienced. You must recognize the devastating impact it has had on her and her children. How has the abuse affected her view of God? She may genuinely love him and desire to please him, but deep inside, she questions his goodness. Does her interpretation of Scripture keep her in bondage? How does she view herself? Is she constantly apologizing? Filled with self-doubt and condemnation? Answers to these questions may not be readily apparent and often take time to determine.

An abused wife has been blamed and condemned for as long as she can remember. Wise counsel will counter what her abuser told her, rather than reinforce it. It assures her that God does not condemn her (Romans 8:1), that he hates what happened to her, and that it actually angers him (Psalm 11:5; Isaiah 58:6–10; Amos 5:21–24). Initial counseling goals should be to provide for safety and stability, then to work to gently restore her relationship with God and help her understand her God-given identity as his daughter.[10] These are merely beginning steps. I pray that this book will inspire you to become even

9. Darby Strickland, *Is It Abuse? A Biblical Guide to Identifying Domestic Abuse and Helping Victims* (Phillipsburg, NJ: P&R, 2020) can help if you are unsure the case is truly abuse. You would also be wise to contact a trained advocate or someone with expertise on domestic abuse.

10. Forrest, *Called to Peace Companion Workbook* contains specific, Scripture-based lessons aimed at restoring to God those who have been oppressed and walking them through the healing process. Lessons can be used by biblical counselors as homework assignments.

more equipped[11] to answer God's call to "loose the chains of injustice and untie the cords of the yoke, to set the oppressed free" (Isaiah 58:6 NIV). Precious lives are hanging in the balance.

11. Called to Peace Ministries offers a one-year advocacy training in conjunction with House of Peace Publications that can help those who desire in-depth training for helping victims (https://www.calledtopeace.org/join-us/become-a-faith-based-advocate/). I also recommend Chris Moles's PeaceWorks University to anyone who desires to help in these situations. You can sign up at www.chrismoles.org.

CHAPTER 5

....

Counseling Goals for Victims of Abuse

Joy Forrest and Darby A. Strickland

When counseling a victim of domestic abuse, there is a great deal to attend to. These cases are often as overwhelming for the counselor as for the counselee. There are a few reasons for this: Victims do not always realize they are being abused. They often seek help for issues like paralyzing anxiety, depression, marital communication, parenting challenges, or other trauma symptoms. Often, they describe themselves as confused rather than abused. That is why helpers need to be alert to the presence of abuse. In addition, we must account for potential safety issues throughout the counseling process. These are so critical that we must address them right away.

Victim care is complex because every victim and her situation are different. She will have brought her own stories, strengths, and weaknesses into the marriage. Does she have children? How many and how old? Does she have a support network, or has she been isolated by her abuse? Further, each victim endures different types and intensities of abuse. Given these realities, victim care must be tailored to each person seeking your help. As we walk you through counseling goals, please remember that this will look different in each and every situation.

Due to the complexities, victim care is long-term care. Counselors, friends, and pastors should adjust their expectations and extend grace and patience as our Lord does with us. God does not tire of repeating himself and pursuing his people. He promises to stay with us for the duration of our suffering journey. We should seek to love victims with the same dedication. Victims of abuse are among the most vulnerable of our counselees.

While we need to execute our role with much wisdom, tenderness, and care, we also need to understand the contours of what we are doing and why we are doing it. This chapter hopes to orient you to the various goals for counseling victims by breaking the counseling into two stages: What does the counselee need in the early days of counseling during the discovery phase? And what are the long-term needs of a victim during the healing phase?

At the outset, we want to encourage you because we know that working with victims is challenging, but it is work that is close to the Lord's heart. In Luke 4, we see the first words of Jesus's public ministry. We hear him reading from the scroll of Isaiah 61, announcing that he came to heal and redeem the damage that sin brings into the world.

> The Spirit of the Lord God is upon me because the LORD has anointed me to bring good news to the poor; he has sent me to bind up the brokenhearted, to proclaim liberty to the captives, and the opening of the prison to those who are bound. (Isaiah 61:1)

If we think about it, this passage can be applied to the vulnerabilities that domestic abuse victims often live with day in and day out—spiritual and potential material poverty, brokenheartedness, and enslavement to their oppressor, but also to their own fear and anxieties as they can become paralyzing. Jesus is not only preaching about the need for deliverance, but he is also telling us that he delivers the oppressed. We are privileged to be a part of Jesus's mission for the vulnerable.

We want to remind you that oppressed wives are enslaved to their husbands; they are not free. Jesus's words about captivity and being bound paint a helpful picture of a victim's reality. Be mindful of that as you walk alongside a victim. Asking her to address the abuse often makes her situation worse at first. Victims often face increased conflicts, further punishments, or new vulnerabilities (economic, social, shared custody) as they speak up, resist, or flee. They will also fear what might happen once they address the abuse. Take time to listen to their concerns and seek to address them. You need to be aware of the reality that fleeing abuse is the most dangerous time for a woman. Women are 70 times more likely to be killed in the first two weeks after leaving than at any other time in their relationship.[1] That is why safety needs to remain a priority no matter where you are in caring for the victim, even if there has been no physical abuse (bodily injury) before separation.

Victim Safety

Throughout your work with a victim, you must be aware of the risks to her safety. A safety assessment and safety plan will need to be done if a basic screening reveals the potential for or presence of violence, stalking, or severe jealousy, or if the victim reports that she fears her husband will harm her. Ideally, in our team approach, the safety assessment should be left to an advocate with specialized training. Sometimes a safety assessment will show that a victim is in danger, and the advocate can help the victim make a detailed safety plan. Some counselors with experience with domestic violence might be able to provide an assessment and safety plan, but it is still wise to involve an advocate when possible. Keep in mind that the level of danger might be so high that drastic measures need to be taken to protect the victim, including finding her a safe location, getting a new

1. Jennifer O'Neill, "Domestic Violence Statistics: The Horrific Reality," *Good Housekeeping*, October 26, 2022, https://www.goodhousekeeping.com/life/relationships/a37005/statistics-about-domestic-violence/.

cell phone free from tracking, or securing an order of protection from the police. There is no room for error or optimism when a victim's safety is at stake. Work with your local shelter or a victim's advocate, or call the National Domestic Hotline.

We use a variety of methods to keep victims safe. Here are some specific measures that should be taken to ensure a victim's safety throughout the process:

- Work under the assumption that her communications are monitored, so be careful what you text and email her.
- Instruct a victim to call the police when physically attacked.
- Since not all victims will choose to leave even when there is danger, teach her how to navigate safety in their home. (For suggestions on this, see appendix A in *Is It Abuse? A Biblical Guide to Identifying Domestic Abuse and Helping Victims* [Phillipsburg, NJ: P & R Publishing, 2020])
- Continually monitor for safety throughout the process; the volatility of the victim's situation often changes, especially after confrontations begin.

Stages of Victim Care

With these foundational principles in place, we can now explore the various counseling goals for victim care. In this chapter, we will not address walking a victim through how to address abuse, as that goal is addressed throughout the book.[2] Instead, we will focus on the counseling goals for the victim. We can only provide you with basic guidelines here, but we hope to alert you to the significant issues that must be addressed. Recognize that these are not necessarily one-and-done phases. There will be overlap and cycling back through them. For example, as we work with victims, sometimes they do not reveal sexual abuse for several months, and then we revisit the discovery phase. And even in the discovery phase of counseling, we still offer

2. For churchwide response, see chapter 2; a counseling response, see chapter 4; an intervention response, see chapter 7; and an advocacy response, see chapter 12.

gospel hope—this aspect of our work does not exclusively belong to the healing phase. We must acknowledge that each of these phases often takes months, if not years. This process cannot be rushed or made to fit a predetermined timetable.

The discovery phase

When you start working with a victim, you must take a substantial amount of time to learn about her story. She will not likely reveal the most severe aspects of the abuse up front. There are a handful of reasons for this. She may not want to dishonor her husband. She may be afraid her husband will find out that she told someone what he has done. She may be minimizing or excusing her husband's behavior and unwilling to admit even to herself the severity of what is happening—saying it out loud makes it more real. Finally, she must trust you enough to share the most intimate details of her life. This trust will come over time as the counselor–counselee relationship develops.

Our goal is to give wise and loving biblical counsel. To accomplish that, you need to know what the victim is enduring and how they cope. I, Darby, find it helpful to remember that I am not just gathering details about someone's story, but tending to a wounded person's body and soul as I learn about what has happened to her. As she talks about the unspeakable things that have happened to her, I want to assist her with speaking to the Lord. So not only do I want to build trust, but I also want to encourage her with the Lord's promises.

Revealing abuse is terrifying. A victim wonders whether she will be believed, if she is accurately assessing what is happening to her, if she will be looked down on, and if she will be supported. Further, when talking about what is happening, victims are usually just beginning to piece together devastating patterns and attitudes. Many victims desperately want help fixing their marriage, but when they start to see the accumulation of pernicious sins and the impacts on them and their children, they become overwhelmed. It often takes them months before they can consistently identify that what is happening to them is abuse. It is a truth that is hard to see, but even harder to accept.

When I witness victims speaking hard truths, revealing shame-filled details, and suffering well, I want to acknowledge the amount of faith and courage it takes to address abuse. It is crucial to be a gentle helper who encourages disclosure but also respects that a victim has their own God-given agency. Victims have been dominated and controlled, so I need to carefully, counsel them on what I see as beneficial while respecting their pace and decisions.

Work to discover the type and extent of abuse that is occurring. In my book, *Is It Abuse?*, I provide hundreds of questions to help you uncover abuse. Why? Because it is essential to get an accurate picture of how a victim is being coercively controlled physically, sexually, emotionally, spiritually, and economically. Every victim's story is different, and we must understand the various contours and intensities. I am continually amazed at the creativity with which people perpetuate evil. You do not want to offer advice or solutions until you understand what a victim is enduring.

Many victims I work with do not identify what is happening to them as abuse. If I ask a victim, "Have you ever been physically abused?" she usually will answer no because she has never been beaten. So I need to break the questions down into specific behaviors: Have you ever been pushed? Slapped? Thrown across the room? Pulled by your hair? When seeking to discover abuse, be careful to craft questions that a victim will not dismiss. Here are a few basic questions:

1. Has your spouse ever hurt you? How?
2. What happens when you disagree with your spouse?
3. Are you afraid to make your spouse angry? Why?
4. Have you ever been an unwilling participant in a sexual act?
5. Do you feel that your input is valued in your relationship? Is your input valued in regard to parenting, money, or how your family spends their time?

6. Do you, at times, feel isolated by your spouse?
7. Do you ever feel afraid of your spouse?
8. Do you have concerns about how your spouse disciplines your children?

These questions are just the beginning. Ask for a few examples to get a sense of what it is like. It is essential to gain enough details so that you feel like you know what it would look like if you were in the room with the victim when the event occurred. Stay curious and ask questions like these: Where was your husband when he said that? What did he look like? What were his hands doing? What did you do? Follow up with more questions, seeking to unearth a story that showcases the highest intensity and to identify what behaviors happen most frequently. Be alert to the fact that many victims will use language that minimizes what has happened (one of the reasons we ask so many questions). Many victims will use mutualizing language that makes them look partially responsible for what happened.

As you are beginning to get a sense of the type of abuse occurring and the intensity of the abuse, it is helpful to work with the victim to make a timeline of her marriage and any abuses she has endured. Because of the trauma she has endured, a victim usually struggles to tell her stories linearly. Part of your role will be to bring order to her confusion and lack of clarity. A timeline will give you a sense of progression and help the victim remember important events. Abuse tends to increase anytime a victim cannot meet all her oppressor's demands. So, ask about what happened after she was ill, had a baby, or faced another tragedy. You will also want to ask about the honeymoon and first year of marriage. Sadly, many of the victims I work with first experienced abuse on their honeymoon or shortly after. They said it was like a flipped switch—once they were married their oppressor knew it was harder for them to flee mistreatment.

Lean how the abuse impacts the sufferer. Many victims' bodies are sending out signals that they are in distress (e.g., migraines, sleeplessness, GI problems, panic attacks). So, ask about any bodily symptoms they may be experiencing. When you find an overwhelmed body, encourage the victim to address their physical suffering. This might mean seeing a doctor or seeking medication to help with paralyzing anxiety or depression. But stay focused on the likely root cause of their bodily symptoms, which is living under abuse and with constant stress. Sometimes a victim needs to flee abuse so that her body can heal; other times she might need a break from the intensity. A victim might be emotionally overloaded or shut down, so try to determine her overall emotional well-being and draw out her heart by giving her a space to talk about and process the abuse, including all the ways it is impacting her and her children. Sometimes you will have to help victims see that what they are enduring is wrong—even evil. Because lamenting a marriage can feel wrong, when a victim can locate what God thinks about abuse of the vulnerable it will give her permission to connect to her own suffering (Psalm 9:18; Psalm 55; Proverbs 6:16–19; Isaiah 3:14–15; Ezekiel 18:12; Amos 2:7; Mark 9:42). Most importantly, check in with the victim about how they are doing spiritually.

Many victims struggle to connect with God and his Word. Sometimes it is because Scripture has been used against them, which can be described as spiritual abuse. Other times it is because they wrongly believe the abuse is their fault or that God has stopped helping them. So, as you unearth abuse, spend significant time reminding victims that the abuse is not their fault and that the Lord sees and cares about what is happening to them (Psalm 146:7–8). Work diligently even in this early stage to connect the sufferer to the Lord. She needs to know that she has his love, care, strength, and help as they consider how to move forward and respond to the abuse.

Thus, as you discover what the abuse is like for the victim and how they are coping, you will also have opportunities to address concerns that are a product of the abuse. Many of these questions and misconceptions can be ministered to even before a victim is willing to address the abuse more globally. During the discovery phase, you can also begin to assess the victim's needs and refer her to additional resources as needed. You might see the need to refer to an advocate (see chapter 12), church care teams, support groups, attorneys, domestic violence agencies, local housing authorities, food banks, and more.

The goal is to not pre-emptively rush to the healing phase—you want to make sure you understand what is going on and ensure that your counselee feels heard and trusts you. Once have assessed your counselee's needs and have a good understanding of the abuse she has endured, as well as the impact it has had on her, you can transition into the next phase and focus more on her healing. Yet, during the healing phase, you may still discover new layers or aspects of the abuse and her responses to it.

The healing phase

If I (Joy) have learned anything in twenty-six years of working with women who have experienced oppression in their marriages, it is that healing is a long, multifaceted process that can be challenging to both the counselor and counselee. I know because I have experienced it from both perspectives. As a victim of abuse, I began to despair to the point that I stopped believing healing was possible. Over time, God miraculously led me through a supernatural healing process based on meditation on Scripture. Years later, as I began counseling women from abusive marriages, I began to share the same truths with them that had set me free. Most of the time, I saw amazing transformations in most of their lives. However, about 25 to 30 percent of them seemed stagnant. After launching our Called to Peace Ministries support groups in 2017, I noticed that women who had experienced a great deal of childhood trauma, particularly childhood sexual abuse, often made far less progress as they worked through the materials. I also saw a small percentage of women without childhood trauma who seemed to struggle more than others.

Addressing trauma first. Just as I found myself growing increasingly perplexed by these women and uncertain about how to best minister to them, books and research began to emerge on the impacts of trauma.[3] I learned that trauma does a significant amount of damage to a person, both body and soul. As the research showed, the effects of trauma are long-lasting.[4] These effects often overwhelm a person. I knew from experience just how true that was. After I got out of my abusive situation, I would tell myself that I was safe and had no reason to panic, but no matter how much I tried, my body seemed to take over without my permission.

As I continued to study trauma, I learned that those who experience it need additional time and care to gain stability. Trauma needs to be addressed both physically and spiritually. I began to recognize that with God's help, I had stumbled onto a process that did just that in my own journey. When I say I healed through meditation on Scripture, I don't mean I repeated or prayed a verse a few times. I mean that I prayed it out loud repeatedly and asked God to implant his truth in my spirit. I sang to him, rocked on my bed, and imagined him holding me as he rejoiced over me with singing (Zephaniah 3:17). My embodied soul needed a process that involved every facet of my being. Within a few years (and yes, note the length of time), I no longer struggled with the symptoms of post-traumatic stress.

Yet, women in our ministry who had genuinely tried to repeat this process remained stuck in their trauma, and I needed to find out why. As I interviewed these women, I found that many had experienced childhood sexual abuse and/or extreme spiritual and sexual abuse in their marriages. Several of them had been married to men in ministry, where Scripture was used to punish and harm them. Approaching the Bible often felt condemning and scary—the opposite of comforting. Most Christian victims of abuse have at least a handful of Scriptures used against them, but for these women, the problem was

---

3. Ed Welch, "Trauma and the Body an Introduction to Three Books," *Journal of Biblical Counseling* 33, no. 2 (2019): 61–83. Here Welch gives a thoughtful review on secular books that have taught us to think carefully about trauma.

4. Lisa M. Shin, Christopher Wright, and Paul Cannistraro, "A Functional Magnetic Resonance Imaging Study of Amygdala and Medial Prefrontal Cortex Responses to Overtly Presented Fearful Faces in Posttraumatic Stress Disorder," (March 2005), Archives of *General Psychiatry*, https://jamanetwork.com/journals/jamapsychiatry/fullarticle/208374.

more extensive. Their view of God and their overwhelming shame prevented them from being able to receive the freeing truth they so desperately needed. This is why it is vitally important for counselors working with victims of abuse to have a foundational understanding of how Scripture is often used as a weapon and the impacts of trauma. To learn more, an excellent starting point is Beth Broom's chapter on trauma in this book (chapter 6) and Darby Strickland's book, *Is It Abuse?*, which covers the traumatic impacts of domestic abuse and the unique impacts of spiritual abuse.

Understanding trauma will give you a solid foundation to help you gently and wisely respond to those who have experienced oppression in their marriages, but it takes time to become skilled in counseling those with trauma—especially in more severe cases. When I meet with victims who are clearly struggling with symptoms of severe post-traumatic stress (so much that it impairs their ability to function in life or benefit from counseling), I usually refer them to counselors who have extensive experience working with traumatized people. This is sometimes just for a season to help them stabilize enough to be able to move forward in the counseling process. For less severe cases, I find that a general knowledge of grounding techniques and meditation on (non-triggering) Scriptures are enough to help counselees begin to heal productively. To facilitate the healing process well, we need to remember that abuse victims have a myriad of challenges and needs. This is why connecting them to resources (with permission) is so important.

Thus, not only must counselors first address safety concerns prior to focusing on our counselees' healing, but we must also deal with severe trauma before moving forward. After this groundwork is laid, there are several key counseling goals that can help shape your conversations with abuse survivors. At the same time, it is essential to remember that healing can look very different for different individuals. It is not a linear process with a clear beginning and end because processing trauma is so complex. You will need to keep that in mind as you may find yourself revisiting issues that seemed settled. The list below contains common themes to be alert for when counseling victims of domestic abuse, but it is not comprehensive.

Key counseling goals during the healing phase

- *Help her identify and reject lies that she has come to believe.* This will include lies she believes about her husband (excuses for the abuse, etc.), lies about her identity (shame, self-blame, etc.), and lies she believes about God (that he does not love her, is not present with her, etc.). Journaling can be a powerful tool in this process.
- *Help her (re)connect with God* by focusing on his goodness, grace, mercy, justice, and any other biblical truths you discern she needs. I was particularly helped by passages that showed God's tender heart toward his children, such as Isaiah 49:14–16, Zephaniah 3:16–17, and Romans 8:15, 31–37.[5]
- *Present healing truths.* This can be done through meditation on Scriptures that help her see the truth without retriggering her trauma. Over time you can gently help her untwist the ones that do.[6]
- *Address overwhelming emotions.* She will need to process grief, anger, fear, and sadness. I explained this process in detail in my book *Called to Peace*, and I listed Scriptures along with helpful questions to help victims process in the *Called to Peace Companion Workbook.*
- *Help her find her identity in Christ.* Most victims have lost sight of their value. She needs to know and internalize who God says she is.

---

5. *Called to Peace* and its companion workbook provide a Scripture database.

6. "When Scriptures Are Used to Oppress—Part 1," Called to Peace Ministries, conversations with Chris Moles, Darby Strickland, and Joy Forrest, October 24, 2019, https://www.youtube.com/watch?v=QRwVnt_ACdo; "When Scriptures Are Used to Oppress—Part 2," Called to Peace Ministries, conversations with Chris Moles, Darby Strickland, and Joy Forrest, October 28, 2019, https://www.youtube.com/watch?v=mUiBoW3P_Ks. These conversations give more information about Scriptures commonly twisted against victims of domestic abuse.

- *Help her move toward forgiveness.* It is crucial that this is not rushed or forced. She needs to understand that forgiveness does not mean she has to trust or reconcile with an unrepentant abuser. It is simply releasing the offender to God, leaving justice to him, and being set free from the burden of unforgiveness. This step was one of the most powerful steps in my own healing process because it took the sting from the abuse memories that had plagued me. This step is extremely difficult, if not impossible, for those who are still being harassed or harmed by their spouses. Generally, it will be a multifaceted process that can take years. For more information on working through forgiveness after abuse, see both the *Called to Peace* book and workbook.
- *Replace unhealthy beliefs and relational patterns with healthy ones.* Without this important step, many (if not most) abuse survivors will find themselves in subsequent abusive marriages as they carry unhealthy patterns from their past into new relationships. This is true even for those who have found significant healing from their trauma.

Conclusion

A victim has been harmed in many ways, and hence there are many things for you to address. Take courage! We have seen the Lord miraculously restore his precious daughters, but it takes time and a willingness to hold out hope again and again for your counselees.

The goal of this chapter is to equip you with a general road map for counseling victims of domestic abuse. Still, because of the complexity of domestic abuse and trauma, those who want to counsel this issue well should commit to additional reading and training. The following are helpful resources for abuse counselors:

- Darby Strickland, *Is It Abuse? A Biblical Guide to Identifying Domestic Abuse and Helping Victims* (Phillipsburg, NJ: P & R Publishing, 20202). A primer on the dynamics of domestic abuse.

- Joy Forrest, *Called to Peace: A Survivor's Guide to Finding Peace and Healing after Domestic Abuse* (Raleigh, NC: Blue Ink Press, 2018) and the *Called to Peace Companion Workbook* (2019). Both give details on the healing process mentioned above.
- Called to Peace Ministries (CTPM) offers advocacy training classes and free seminars on domestic abuse through its church partnership program.
- Christian Healing Trauma Network offers webinars and training on understanding and responding to trauma.

We pray that this chapter has inspired you to learn more. Your willingness to learn and walk alongside those who are being oppressed will make all the difference in the world for those who have very likely forgotten the love and goodness of our God.

CHAPTER 6

....

Trauma Healing for Abuse Survivors

Beth M. Broom, LPC-S, CCTP-II

Regardless of the type of abuse or the length of time it has occurred, a victim of abuse will bear the scars of traumatization. She cannot come out of these experiences unscathed. She has been robbed of her dignity and agency so she will be left with the painful work of rebuilding those parts of her personhood. Fortunately for those who are children of God, the work is empowered by the Holy Spirit and designed by divine providence and timing. But the work cannot be done alone. She needs advocates and wise counselors to guide her on the journey.

How do we conceptualize trauma and its effects? It seems as though *trauma* has become something of a cultural buzzword these days, to the extent that some people believe any negative event can cause someone to be traumatized. We need a comprehensive definition of *traumatization* so that it doesn't become watered down or inflated.

The Substance Abuse and Mental Health Services Administration (SAMHSA) defines *trauma* as "an event or circumstance resulting in physical harm, emotional harm and/or life-threatening harm. The event or circumstance has lasting adverse effects on the individual's mental, physical, and emotional health, as well as on social and/or spiritual well-being."[1] There are two elements to this definition: the events and the effects of the events. A person can experience harmful events without suffering lasting adverse effects from those events. However, with abuse, the harmful events and their effects almost always constitute traumatization. Therefore, it's important for us to understand what happens in the body and the mind when trauma occurs because this will give us greater understanding and compassion for the victim as she struggles with symptoms of traumatization.

What Happens in the Mind and Body When Trauma Occurs?

Traumatization's effects on the mind and body have been studied extensively in the field of neuroscience over the past several years, and the results have given insight into what actually happens when the fight/flight response is activated.[2] This is important for us to learn because victims of abuse have experienced drastic fight/flight responses during the course of traumatization, and these responses have shaped their long-term patterns of thought, emotions, and behavior.

The fight/flight system becomes activated in any dangerous situation. You do not have to calculate what to do when you encounter the threat of harm—your brain secretes hormones that cause your body to do the heavy lifting so you can get away from danger or fight against it. Rational thought takes a back seat when this system is activated because self-preservation is the higher goal. The body kicks into high gear, causing elevated heart rate, muscle tension, and shortness of breath. Digestive function decreases in order to give greater energy to the body's extremities.

---

1. "Trauma and Violence," Substance Abuse and Mental Health Services Administration, last modified September 27, 2022, https://www.samhsa.gov/trauma-violence.

2. Bessel van der Kolk, *The Body Keeps the Score: Brain, Mind, and Body in the Healing of Trauma* (New York: Penguin Publishing Group, 2015); Robert Scaer, *Trauma Spectrum* (New York: W. W. Norton & Company, 2005); Joseph LeDoux, *Anxious: Using the Brain to Treat Fear and Anxiety* (New York: Penguin Publishing Group, 2015); Babette Rothschild, *Revolutionizing Trauma Treatment: Stabilization, Safety, and Nervous System Balance* (New York: W. W. Norton & Company, 2021). These resources give more information about the research in neuroscience.

Once the threat of harm subsides, the body is designed to return to equilibrium. Heart rate decreases, breathing goes back to normal, and rational decision-making is reactivated. But those who have experienced trauma remain in a state of bodily hyperarousal. And when a person lives in a continually dangerous situation like domestic violence, the fight/flight system is running pretty constantly. It's not difficult to understand why abuse victims often have trouble relaxing, sleeping, or concentrating.

If you'll forgive the oversimplification of one of God's most complex, creative designs, let me give you a tangible way to understand what's happening in the mind. Think of the mind like an intricate and interconnected filing system that includes my memories, knowledge, and social experiences. Every time I encounter a situation, I pull a "file" (or several files) to help me determine how I should respond. I gather information from previous situations in order to decide how to handle the current situation.

Sometimes this happens very quickly without conscious thought. For example, when I'm standing in the street talking to my neighbor and see a car coming toward me at a fast pace, my mind quickly recalls what I should do next. I don't have to calculate anything—I simply turn and run toward the sidewalk. This form of memory is called "procedural memory," and it activates quickly without conscious thought in order to provide a speedy result. The brain creates an equation that says "If _______, then _______." This equation is meant to simplify and accelerate action.

If I encounter a traumatic event, procedural memory is created. But this type of procedural memory is intensely strong because of its attachment to the fight/flight response. I anticipate danger with great vigilance because my mind remembers the previous consequences of that danger, so my body will respond to the threat of harm with energy and force in order to prevent damage from happening again. These are automatic responses to a threat of harm, created to help keep a person safe.

It's important to note that a *potential* threat of harm registers just as strongly as an *actual* threat of harm for a victim of abuse because she carries procedural memory of the danger, the result of that danger, and what she has to do to prevent it. This is essential for us to understand because otherwise we run the risk of blaming victims or minimizing their fears. We may think they are overreacting to things that aren't really dangerous while their minds are simply registering danger and responding accordingly. We will not successfully talk someone out of feeling hypervigilant about danger because rational thought has taken the back seat behind the bodily functions that are seeking to keep her safe. Wisdom dictates that we seek to help return her body to a relative state of calm so that she can see situations with clarity and make healthy decisions. We'll return to this concept later in the chapter.

What Are the Symptoms of Traumatization?

Those who have experienced traumatization are often dealing regularly with intrusions, avoidance, absolutism, changes in mood and demeanor, and changes in arousal and reactivity. And yet there is hope for them to find peace! Let's explore each of these challenges that our counselees encounter.

Intrusions

For those who have experienced a traumatizing event or season of life, the past is not simply in the past. Intrusions happen when a person suddenly reexperiences the emotions, sensations, and thoughts of a traumatic moment. Common examples include flashbacks and nightmares, but another form of intrusion happens when the body ramps up (called hyperarousal) or shuts down (called hypoarousal) as a thought, image, or emotion intrudes. Suddenly the survivor is right back in the same bodily state she experienced during a traumatizing event.

This is a maddening experience. The survivor never knows what might cause an intrusion, and she has no way to gauge how her body will respond when the moment hits. What's worse, her friends and loved ones often don't understand what she's experiencing. They may say or do things in reaction to her intrusions that can cause her to feel shamed and disbelieved, thus leading her toward further isolation and loneliness.

Avoidance

A victim may avoid memories, thoughts, feelings, and situations associated with a traumatic event. This may include people, places, conversations, activities, or objects. For example, I counseled a woman who avoided a certain part of town for years because a terrifying incident occurred there. She felt certain she was going to be endangered simply by going there. Again, this avoidance is not based on rational thought. I would not have been able to convince her that she was safe from harm because that event was buried deep in her procedural memory.

Often victims feel embarrassed and frustrated by this avoidance. They are aware that their avoidance is not rational or objective, and they wish they could just make themselves think differently. This avoidance can also significantly decrease daily functioning and cause consequences if a victim senses the need to avoid things that cannot be avoided without significant repercussions, like social interactions or driving a car.

Absolutism

When chaos occurs, a person seeks to find clear and simple answers in order to move forward. Trauma survivors often think in terms of absolutism: beliefs that are extreme and polarized. Examples include thoughts such as, *The world is completely unsafe*, *No one can be trusted*, and *All men are dangerous.* While absolutism is not unique to traumatization, it almost always occurs when a person has been traumatized.

Unfortunately, the simplest answers that help us cope with trauma often form beliefs that wind up hindering our flourishing in the long run. If the world seems completely unsafe for a victim, her solution to that problem may be to stay home and never take risks. You can see how this form of coping would isolate a person and potentially damage relationships.

Changes in mood and demeanor

Often those who have been traumatized struggle to feel hopeful and happy. Understandably, their worlds have turned upside down with no sense of when or how things will be back to normal again. I have worked with trauma survivors who had been diagnosed with depression or anxiety before meeting with me, but their diagnoses had not considered the toll trauma had taken on their ability to function. While traumatization may include depression or anxiety (or both), the key lies in the root of the suffering. If a person's depressed or anxious mood begins as a result of a traumatizing event or season of life, the trauma will need to be healed in order for the struggles with depression or anxiety to be helped.

Trauma survivors may also experience detachment or isolation from others. The experience of trauma is very lonely, and the survivor can feel as if she is a burden. I've heard survivors say that they believe their friends are tired of their suffering or that they are causing other people to be depressed because of their depression. So their solution is often to pull away from loved ones. Inevitably, the suffering worsens when the sufferer is alone. This can become a vicious downward spiral.

Changes in arousal and reactivity

As we discussed earlier, the body becomes highly alert and reactive when the fight/flight system is activated. If a person does not come back to a state of equilibrium after a traumatizing event, her arousal response will remain active. Hypervigilance is the most obvious of these symptoms. The victim stays in a constant state of watchfulness, fully expecting something awful to happen at any moment. It's a terrible way to live, but it's the experience of many trauma survivors. Other common symptoms include problems with concentration and an exaggerated startle response.

These struggles with hyperarousal and reactivity don't affect only the survivor of trauma, but also relationships are affected when the survivor is prone to outbursts of anger or irritability. We do not excuse sinful behavior, but it's helpful to understand the factors that can play into that behavior. So when a person expects to be harmed at any given moment, it might make sense that she yells out in anger when she's startled by someone dropping a dish.

If this list of symptoms seems overwhelming to you, I encourage you to remember the truth: nothing that has been shattered is beyond redemption and healing. With our God, all things are possible (Matthew 19:26). Listen to the words of Isaiah 61:1–4:

> The Spirit of the Lord God is upon me,
>   because the Lord has anointed me
> to bring good news to the poor;
>   he has sent me to bind up the brokenhearted,
> to proclaim liberty to the captives,
>   and the opening of the prison to those who are bound;
> to proclaim the year of the Lord's favor,
>   and the day of vengeance of our God;
>   to comfort all who mourn;
> to grant to those who mourn in Zion—
>   to give them a beautiful headdress instead of ashes,
> the oil of gladness instead of mourning,
>   the garment of praise instead of a faint spirit;
> that they may be called oaks of righteousness,
>   the planting of the Lord, that he may be glorified.
> They shall build up the ancient ruins;
>   they shall raise up the former devastations;
> they shall repair the ruined cities,
>   the devastations of many generations.

These prophetic words point to our Savior, who made himself nothing in order that we may become a holy and beloved people belonging to God. Hope abounds for the children of God.

How Should We Care for Survivors of Trauma?

Imagine with me for a moment what it must have been like to be a follower of Jesus during his earthly ministry. Everywhere he went, people begged him for healing. Crowds gathered in every town to listen to his wise words. His disciples left everything to follow him. Isaiah 53:2 says, "he had no form or majesty that we should look at him, and no beauty that we should desire him." By earthly standards, he wasn't noticeable. But there was something about him that drew people in and gave them hope.

The first and most important way in which we should care for survivors of trauma is by imitating how Jesus cared for people in his earthly ministry and how he continues to care for us as he sits at the right hand of the Father: he is *fully present.* He calls those who are weary and burdened to come to him and find rest for their souls (Matthew 11:28–30).

The ministry of presence

Jesus didn't hurry. In every situation, he paid attention to the people who were in front of him. He wasn't driven by what needed to happen next or by people's history of sin and suffering. He was perfectly able to receive someone as they were in the moment. His love and acceptance caused others to feel safe and loved, which allowed them to trust him with their healing and growth.

No matter what method or technique we may use in helping guide people toward healing from trauma, the attitude of our hearts must be to approach others as unique beings made in God's image. We must see them as worthy of honor and dignity. And we cannot have this attitude if we are driven by the future or the past.

Being driven by the future often looks like listening to someone only long enough to get sufficient information to provide a solution. Some of us are good problem-solvers and seem to have a knack for discerning the pitfalls that lie ahead. These are highly valuable gifts, but they must not be the first gifts we utilize.

The initial goal must always be serving as a compassionate presence, a willingness to learn and bear witness. If you find yourself hurrying toward solutions when someone is sharing her struggle, I want to encourage you to slow down. The person in front of you is complex—you will not be able to map out her past, present, and future life even if you spend every hour of every day with her. She belongs to God, and he is her shepherd on this journey. This truth frees you to patiently come alongside and travel at a slower pace.

We can also be pulled out of the present moment when we are compelled to "figure out" a person's struggle by investigating every element of her traumatic history. I notice myself doing this when I feel stuck as a counselor. I somehow think that if I can put together the puzzle of a person's past, I can figure out how to map out the journey of healing. But it doesn't work like this. While a person's story is very important, it's not important because it tells me how to heal her wounds; it's important because it belongs to her. It has shaped how she thinks about the world, herself, and God. It's an element of who she is, but it's only one of many elements. She most needs me to join her and point her toward the Lord, not to figure her out. She is a person to love, not a problem to be solved.

I want to encourage you to talk with the Lord about the concept of being fully present. You may not even know you're hurrying toward future solutions or overanalyzing the past. Many of us have been trained to do these things, so it could be a tough habit to break. Ask the Lord to search you and know your heart. What motivates you as you walk alongside trauma survivors? What fears may be compelling you toward the future or the past, keeping you from being fully present with people? As you reflect, you'll actually be practicing the very thing that will make you a good counselor—slowing down, listening, and joining the Father in his work.

I'm not going to offer a list of specific skills for being fully present because I don't want you to create a behavioral checklist. But you can ask people in your life to share ways they sense you are fully present with them, as well as ways they notice you being pulled into the future or the past. Hopefully you have honest friends and loved ones who will tell you what they see in you. I have done this exercise, and it's very eye-opening! A family member has told me that he can tell just by how I'm sitting and breathing that I'm hurrying to the next thing on my list rather than being present with him. I have a friend who told me that I start to speak in short sentences when I'm thinking about something else rather than what she's saying. As you might imagine, this exercise is not for the faint of heart, but it will serve you well.

Your ministry of presence with a survivor of trauma will be essential throughout the relationship. It doesn't mean you won't ever challenge her toward setting goals and building new patterns of thought and behavior. As you show up to be with her on this journey, she will feel safe enough to take risks. She will see you as an advocate and trustworthy guide, rather than someone who just wants to change her. And most importantly, you will be emulating your Savior and communicating his love to her.

The ministry of stabilization

You'll remember that traumatization causes struggles with body stabilization, negative thoughts, and alterations in mood. Often survivors of trauma are unaware or neglectful of these symptoms, and they may not have tools for managing them. So it's really important for us as helpers to pay attention to what's happening. When we notice a person's physical and emotional state and then point out what we notice, she will be more able to attend to her own responses and calm any feelings of being overwhelmed.

We could easily fill an entire chapter with tools for helping a person stabilize. But since we can only talk briefly about this topic here, I'll give some very practical exercises you can do with someone who needs to stabilize her body and mind. First, taking deep breaths will help calm the body's automatic responses of fight/flight. There's not a specific formula that always works—the goal is simply to breathe slowly and deeply. As she does this, you invite her to notice where she feels tension in her body and focus her mental energy on relaxing those muscles. In doing this, she is also diverting mental energy away from whatever has caused the feelings of being overwhelmed.

The body is filled with energy when the fight/flight response is activated. Breathing deeply helps decrease heart rate, but the energy created by the hormones released during fight/flight response may still be trapped in the body. After some deep breaths, I'll often invite the person to tense and relax particular muscles in the body to help release this energy. For example, we might interlock our fingers and squeeze hard for five seconds, followed by releasing the fingers and shaking them out while taking a deep breath. Another option is to push the palms of the hands against a wall, like doing a standing push-up, followed by releasing and shaking out the arms and legs. It is helpful in itself to do these exercises, but we also want to engage the mind by asking, "What does it feel like in your fingers when you press them together? What does it feel like when you release them and shake them out?" These questions invite the person to verbalize what she is experiencing, thus activating the language center of the brain and helping bring the mind back into full functioning.

Keep in mind that you need to do these exercises with her, not just explain to her what she should do. This is part of the stabilization process. You are joining her so that she understands your connection to what she is experiencing. Counselees have told me that they felt so embarrassed at being overwhelmed, but that their embarrassment vanished as I joined them in calming the body.

The *freeze* response is an important aspect of being overwhelmed. When a person's mind anticipates that she will not be able to fight or flee, the freeze response can be activated. You may notice that a person shuts down bodily or mentally, and it seems she is no longer listening or functioning. If this happens, give her some space. State out loud what you notice by saying, "It seems you have gone somewhere else. I'm here, and I'm ready to be with you in whatever you're experiencing." Then wait a few seconds and watch for movement. Once she begins to reengage with you, you can ask her what she experienced and offer to talk through it. If she remains disengaged for more than about thirty seconds, invite her to do something small like wiggle her toes inside her shoes or tap her fingers against her legs. Small movements like this can help bring the body and mind back into the present moment.

If the freeze response happens often during your conversations, you will want to consult with a professional counselor who is trained in trauma care. Frequent freeze responses may indicate that a person's mind is unable to handle the topics you are discussing, causing an overload of sorts. Trauma professionals are trained in how and when to engage in the healing work, as well as how and when to slow down and redirect a person who is not yet ready to process the pain.

The ministry of wisdom

James 1:5 says, "If any of you lacks wisdom, let him ask God, who gives generously to all without reproach, and it will be given him." God does not withhold wisdom from us. He is eager to give it generously to anyone who asks. I think we can all agree that counseling ministry requires ample doses of wisdom, but I'm not sure we talk enough about how to gain wisdom and walk in it.

One of my favorite verses as a trauma counselor is Ecclesiastes 7:4: "The heart of the wise is in the house of mourning." I quote this verse to my counselees because I want them to grow in understanding the importance of what I call "walking all the way around our suffering." Sometimes a counselee will share her struggle with me and then hope I can give her a formula for how to heal or improve the situation. I won't do this because she is not a machine that simply needs to be fixed. Honoring her means that I don't offer formulas.

Many people share only minimal details and exclude the emotion of their experiences because they feel afraid that they won't be able to manage the feelings that arise. I must take plenty of time to get to know a person's story and perspective. I pay attention to her emotions, words, and bodily responses. If she's able to stay relatively stabilized while sharing, I invite her to walk around this house of mourning with me.

Entering the house of mourning means I want to know her experience of grief, not just the story of the grievous thing that happened. I want to learn the emotions that come with the story as well as the thoughts and beliefs that have shaped her. I want her to name and describe her reality without sugarcoating or minimizing its effects. So I'll regularly remind counselees that they don't need to give me "Sunday school answers" or quickly slap biblical truth on a hard situation.

People need to let themselves feel and express pain. This is a very difficult thing to do for many survivors of trauma. It can seem really dangerous. As a way to help counselees understand the process, I often point to David as an example of entering the house of mourning. In many of the psalms, David begins with a question that is filled with grief and anger. He articulates his pain and shares his experience with God. As this happens, he begins to see more clearly. He expresses God's goodness and righteousness as the truth comes into view, and he receives comfort and hope. (For examples of this process, see Psalms 22, 38, 55, and 88.)

As we name and feel the experience of pain in front of our loving God, we are asking him to join us. He draws near to us and provides comfort for our pain. Then healing begins as we are able to see his love in the midst of our suffering. As you can probably imagine, this process does not happen quickly. Here's how it usually goes in my process with a trauma survivor:

First, I give her space to share her experience with me. I sometimes have to prompt her to share more than just events. I want to hear her experience—the thoughts, feelings, relational dynamics, and sensations that come with the suffering. If she tries to minimize her pain, diverts into excusing the wounds, or compare her pain to that of someone else, I gently refocus her attention on the experience itself. Then I give validation to the hurt. I express how I feel about her suffering, including both sadness and anger at the difficulty she has endured.

Next, I ask some questions about what she has come to believe as a result of the suffering she experienced. How did this experience shape her beliefs about herself, other people, the world, and God? We spend time exploring these things, as if we're walking slowly through all the rooms of the house. I have been amazed at the ways God has brought clarity and wisdom to counselees when they explore these questions. They begin to talk about their suffering without so much shame and self-blame. Again, this takes a lot of time.

The most frequent question my counseling students ask is, "How do I know when to help a person leave the house of mourning and start walking ahead?" I don't have a specific answer to this question because every person's process is unique. But here are three things I recommend to help discern when it's time to leave the house of mourning:

- *Pray.* Jesus listened to the voice of the Father to know what to say and do, and we must follow his example. Ask God to show you wisdom every step of the way.
- *Listen for hints from the counselee.* She will begin to say truthful things about herself, God, and others as she grieves. For example, she may go from saying an event was all her fault to stating that she could not have prevented it. She may begin to talk about God the way David does in the Psalms—not as a diversion from her pain, but as a way of reminding herself who he is.

- *Consult with wise people.* We are never meant to do this work in isolation. Befriend at least two or three wise counselors with whom you can collaborate. Sharing ideas with each other is a great source of wisdom.

Finally, we begin to discuss how she wants the experience to shape her life. We can't help but be shaped by the things and people we encounter, but we can ask God to give us his perspective. We can look forward to what's next in our lives as the wounds of our past are healed. And the house of mourning can become a familiar space we return to as needed. I have found that trauma survivors have moments—and even seasons—when they need to mourn losses they have mourned before. It's all part of the journey.

Growing in Your Ability to Care Well

Caring for survivors of trauma is a complex and long-term process. This chapter is a primer of sorts, but perseverance in this kind of ministry requires some additional tools. I want you to be strengthened throughout the work so that you can continue for the long haul. Let's look at some ways you can become better equipped.

Self-awareness

If you are caring for survivors of trauma, you must be prepared to see yourself clearly and give yourself grace for the journey. Helpers need help as well, so make some trusted and wise friends who will pray for you and support you. I even encourage the counselors I supervise to have a counselor of their own who they check in with regularly. Hebrews 10:24–25 says, "And let us consider how to stir up one another to love and good works, not neglecting to meet together, as is the habit of some, but encouraging one another, and all the more as you see the Day drawing near." We may have become proficient at encouraging others, but we also need to be willing and even eager to receive encouragement from others.

It's important to set aside regular times to gauge how you're doing and what you need in order to continue to pour into others. When the work is heavy, it's easy to ignore our own needs and weaknesses. Who is asking you good questions about how you're taking care of yourself? Who knows when you are feeling weak or burdened? When is it time to slow down and receive? These are questions you will need help to answer because you won't always see yourself clearly.

Additional training and consultation

As you care for trauma survivors, you will encounter unique situations that require specific types of care. Remember that you won't know exactly what to do for a person even if you know everything about her story, so befriend wise counselors who are experienced in this type of work and then make plans to spend time with them. Keep in mind the words of Proverbs 24:5–6: "A wise man is full of strength, and a man of knowledge enhances his might, for by wise guidance you can wage your war, and in abundance of counselors there is victory."

While information alone cannot help people heal from their trauma, we should always be growing. The more you can understand about the effects of trauma and the methods you can use to help people heal, the more you'll be equipped to effectively walk alongside survivors. Some dear friends and I have created Christian Trauma Healing Network, a non-profit organization that equips helpers with content and collaboration. You can find us at www.christiantrauma healingnetwork.org.

Reliance on the Good Shepherd

Above all else, we must keep our eyes fixed on Jesus. He is our Savior, our healer, and our Wonderful Counselor. He knows what we need and how to move us forward in sanctification. He's familiar with our weakness, and he understands the thoughts and motives of our hearts. Without him, we will be blind counselors leading other blind people into futility.

How is your relationship with the Lord? Are you abiding in him? Are you connected to his body, the church? We all experience times of weakness and drought. But if you are malnourished in your faith, you will not be able to serve others in a healthy way. Some helpers will keep doing the work and ignore their own faith struggles because they believe they have to put the needs of others above their own. I assure you that the Lord has not asked us to run ourselves into the ground for the sake of ministry. Many counselors, pastors, and lay leaders have faltered into pervasive sin and despair when they refused to acknowledge their own needs.

I am so grateful that you are reading this book because it means your heart longs for the health and healing of abuse survivors. May the Lord continue to strengthen and grow you, and may you rest in the power of his Spirit to provide everything you need for the journey.

CHAPTER 7

....

Caring for Families by Confronting Abusers

Chris Moles

I wasn't quite accustomed to my new environment, but I had positioned myself the best I could in order to see and interact with each man in the room—I was leaning on a nearby windowsill facing the uneven rows of chairs. The occasion was a group-facilitated discussion for abusive men, and this evening we had been relocated to a second-floor lobby due to some confusion over room reservations in the facility. While we were exploring the men's choices, actions, and impacts on their partners, one gentleman became visibly agitated with my questions and persistence. I took a moment to address him personally and press into his discomfort: "What are you thinking about?" The man looked at me intensely, and without hesitation he balked and said, "I'm thinking about throwing you out that window." Now, I would contend that this may have indeed been an empty threat, but he did have a history of physical violence and was already in trouble with the law for a few altercations, including some with other men. In that moment, I held up my hand and asked him to hold that thought.

I quickly moved to another wall with no windows, but I mimicked my exact posture as before, only now I was leaning safely against the wall. Then I repeated my question: "Now what are you thinking?" He sighed and shook his head, the group began to chuckle, and we continued our discussion. Intervening with abusive men may be as much an art form as a procedure, if not more so. Escalation, hostility, attempts at collusion, playing the role of the victim, and a variety of other strategies may be employed to avoid or reduce accountability.

Having Hard Conversations

It's never easy to have conversations about your sin, especially when that sin involves harming, demeaning, or controlling your partner. That is, however, what is required in cases of domestic abuse. We must confront abusers in order to not only care well for their own souls but also to protect and care for those who have been abused. Before we look specifically at a biblical approach to conducting these conversations, I'd like to offer a couple of best practices to help you prepare for and understand the complexities of such interventions.

First, when possible, seek victim consent before proceeding. If you witness an act of violence, it may require an immediate response, but if you have received a disclosure from the victim, it is best to first connect her to local resources (if desired), such as a shelter, law enforcement, and a qualified counselor or advocate to address her immediate needs before you speak with her about a possible intervention with her husband. It is also important to ensure that she has a proper safety plan in place. Speaking to her partner without consent or proper safety planning may place her in additional danger and escalate the risk of harm.

Second, consider the value of a team-based approach to care. Assembling a community around the victim and her partner increases accountability and provides for additional safety. A counselor, advocate, and access to community-based resources can serve the victim well. Enlisting sources of accountability for the abuser, such as mentors, trained counselors, and perhaps a batterer intervention and prevention group or enrollment in the Men of Peace self-paced course[1] can provide the abuser with the education and oversight he needs.

1. Chris Moles, "Men of Peace Self-Paced Course," Men of Peace, accessed December 10, 2022, https://www.menofpeace.org/.

Once these preliminary steps have been taken, we must prepare for the hard conversations involved in an intervention by turning to the Scriptures. What biblical principles should we aim to keep in mind as we speak with an abuser? One Scripture that has served me well in addressing abusers and training others to do so has been Galatians 6:1–10 (NIV).

> Brothers and sisters, if someone is caught in a sin, you who live by the Spirit should restore that person gently. But watch yourselves, or you also may be tempted. Carry each other's burdens, and in this way you will fulfill the law of Christ. If anyone thinks they are something when they are not, they deceive themselves. Each one should test their own actions. Then they can take pride in themselves alone, without comparing themselves to someone else, for each one should carry their own load. Nevertheless, the one who receives instruction in the word should share all good things with their instructor. Do not be deceived: God cannot be mocked. A man reaps what he sows. Whoever sows to please their flesh, from the flesh will reap destruction; whoever sows to please the Spirit, from the Spirit will reap eternal life. Let us not become weary in doing good, for at the proper time we will reap a harvest if we do not give up. Therefore, as we have opportunity, let us do good to all people, especially to those who belong to the family of believers.

From this passage I have derived the following biblical principles that shape how I approach an intervention. My prayer is that you also find them helpful the next time you need to prepare for one of these hard conversations.

The Goal of an Intervention: Restoration (v. 1)

We counsel with an agenda. We are, after all, ministers of reconciliation according to 2 Corinthians 5:11–21. Interventions conducted well and by experienced and skilled counselors can help the church more aggressively and accurately understand the extent of the sin of abuse, the tremendous needs of repentance, and the necessary elements of forgiveness. Please note that our primary objective is to restore people to God. I bring this up because I have noted that in the church, there frequently seems to be a desire to grant forgiveness quickly, not always on the basis of faith or a robust understanding of biblical forgiveness, but rather on the basis of convenience or institutional comfort. Abused wives are often encouraged to prematurely reconcile with abusive husbands, and congregations have been encouraged to return abusive leaders to ministry.

Thus, we must approach the hard conversations involved in an intervention with purpose, and one of those key purposes is to restore sinners to God, not to their formerly held positions, institutions, or reputations. So how are we to restore abusers to God? We must start with understanding the problem clearly. One key element of biblical counseling is the foundational commitment to evaluating problems biblically. In cases of domestic abuse, far too often the issues involved have been reduced to marriage problems, which have led to rushed attempts to reconcile the marriage. However, the problem of abuse is not mutual—it is a one-sided use of power to dominate or control. Therefore, an intervention must specifically address the abuser's heart and mind. The greatest weapon we have against domestic abuse is changing the hearts of the abusers. This entails having difficult but gospel-centered conversations that call abusive men to repent and be restored to God, whether their marriage is salvageable or not.

The People Conducting an Intervention: A Mature Response (v. 1)

It is important to note that in Galatians 6, the ones responsible for conducting an intervention are those who live by the Spirit. Paul is referring here to mature Christians who are bearing the fruit of the Spirit. I bring this up because it communicates that this kind of confrontational ministry is not a task to be undertaken alone, especially for novice biblical counselors or inexperienced pastors. It is therefore imperative that one continue their education in domestic abuse care beyond an isolated, single book or lecture. Domestic abuse contains a variety of complexities, and there are many temptations present in confronting abusers, as Galatians 6:1 indicates. For instance, when training pastors on the dynamics of domestic abuse, I have frequently heard them suggest the strategy of "bullying the bully." This approach entails showing up to the abuser's home with multiple deacons, usually larger men, in order to intimidate or threaten the abuser into better behavior. The problem is that such approaches reinforce the very worldview we are combating—the idea that strength and power should be used to threaten others to produce the desired behavior. No, our response must be different and should be conducted by individuals who are mature and grounded in their faith and committed to the process. In addition to having mature faith, seasoned biblical counselors who are trained in the dynamics and impact of abuse will be better situated to engage abusers.

The Means Used in an Intervention: Gentleness (v. 1)

In the previous section, I described how we might be tempted to mirror the abuser's demeanor, worldview, or behavior in our confrontation of them. In contrast, the Bible clearly calls us to a posture of gentleness. If I'm stepping into a manipulative, controlling, angry, rage-filled, demeaning person's life to call them to repent of their sin, the temptation for me is to become angry, rage-filled, manipulative, controlling, and demeaning. I've not found that to be a successful strategy or consistent with Scripture. To restore a sinner requires that I model for them how I expect them to treat others. *Gentleness* does not mean soft or suggest a lack of resolve. In fact, gentleness as practically applied to one's life will more than likely view our own position or power as a means to serve others rather than a weapon to cause them harm. Gentleness positions us in stark contrast to the abusive person. We are not coercive or demeaning; rather, we use our strength and position to call him to repentance. A pithy but effective phrase that I've been using when training counselors is "we hit hard in safe places." In other words, we speak hard, solid truth in winsome ways. No, we don't let up—the consequences are still in place, and the boundaries are still in place—but we must maintain gentleness as our posture. After all, it is God who grants repentance, and any notion that we are in some way coercing repentance is dangerous. It is God's kindness that leads us to repentance (Romans 2:4). We can only invite people to repent. We can participate in seeking justice, but God brings about the fruit of the intervention.

Individuals may respond by either turning from their sin in repentance or by remaining obstinate and overtly or covertly rejecting our call. Then, based on the decisions they make, we have an obligation to move forward. I've worked with many churches that belabor this process. They lengthen the process in the hopes that they will eventually be able to bring about repentance and reconciliation, but stretching out the process generally serves the abuser and is often a detriment to the victims. I am not speaking of a man who rejects a truth on Friday only to accept that same truth on Monday following self-reflection and conviction. That is a wonderful outcome. I am speaking of extending our hopes of repentance by weeks, months, or years in spite of a husband's continued attempts at reframing our counsel, rejecting our counsel, and overwhelming or attempting to manipulate the counselors.

A Brief Warning to Church Leaders

The Bible is chock-full of interventions, beginning with God intervening on our behalf in Genesis 3.[2] In the book of Exodus, we see

2. Genesis 3:8–24 records God's response to the fall, which includes the confrontation of Adam and Eve, the promise of future redemption, as well as an explanation of the consequences of sin entering the world.

Jethro intervene to help Moses manage the people.[3] And Matthew 18 has often been used as a model of how interventions should be done in the church. Pastors and churches who step into cases of domestic abuse will often rely heavily on Matthew 18 to guide their approach. We know that this New Testament framework for intervention begins when a brother or a sister comes alongside a sinning brother or sister to confront their sin and call them to repentance. If the sinner remains unrepentant, the process will culminate in the church's excommunication of the unrepentant sinner. It's important to note that Matthew 18 is a process that, in cases of domestic abuse, began when the wife first confronted the abuser. This is a key point because many leaders that I've spoken with need help properly plotting where they actually are in the process. Some pastors fail to recognize that the leaders' confrontation of the husband is much closer to the end of church discipline process than the beginning.

Let's say a wife discloses abuse in the home and she has tried nearly every avenue available to her to call her husband to repentance, but the sin remains in their relationship, causing continued harm and fear. The church intervenes and engages the spouses in individual counseling, while calling the husband to repentance. But throughout the process he vacillates, only to continue various forms of the abuse, resist real change, and even blame his spouse or play the victim. At this point, churches will seek my help and say that they are preparing to begin church discipline according to Matthew 18. However, I would contend that the church and the victim are nearing the end of the Matthew 18 process. She has confronted him, sought help from the church, and that help has been rejected or manipulated. Why would we begin a process that has already revealed the abuser's heart?

3. Exodus 18:13–27 is the story of Moses's father-in-law, Jethro, helping Moses recognize his need for help in judging and ruling on the concerns of the people.

The Goal of an Intervention: Ownership (v. 5)

Paul tells us that during our Galatians 6 intervention, everyone should carry their own load. Although we are coming alongside an individual caught in sin, the context of this passage would lead me to believe that the "burden bearing" we are engaged in is in regard to sin and perhaps our intervention is doing just that, sharing the load of recognizing and repenting. Mature believers therefore have responsibilities in the process, to confront others in an attempt to call them to take responsibility for their own sin. This may sound obvious, but abusive individuals tend to minimize their own choices, deny their actions outright, or shift the blame to their partner, a substance, a mental health condition, or give any number of excuses. Ownership is a key point within the intervention, and if the person we are confronting will not own their sin, then we have little to offer them moving forward in regard to change or hope.

The Results of an Intervention: Consequences and God's Glory (vv. 7–8)

The bottom line of an intervention is that Christ is doing the work, and a person's soul is at stake as we fulfill the mandate of Galatians chapter 6. The reality of our work is that someone we are called to care for is caught in a devastating pattern of sin, one in which he uses power and position to control his partner. We know that such behavior will lead to devastating consequences, such as great harm to his wife and family as well as potential consequences for himself. Confrontational ministry is a gift of grace in this man's life, inviting him to repent, to recognize his own corrupt worldview, and to embrace the hope found in the gospel. If he chooses to repent, then God is glorified through this man's transformation, growth, and change. If he chooses to reject our warnings, then God is glorified through our faithfulness to protect this man's wife and children by supporting and even participating in the potential consequences before him, including police involvement, church discipline, divorce, etc. So this process is an exercise in growing in greater dependence upon Jesus. This process should be strengthening everyone involved, from the people doing the confronting to the individual being confronted. And, of course the victim should be experiencing the freedom to continue growing in grace and in dependence upon Christ.

We glorify God when we represent him as his ambassadors. The result of our intervention can be peace as we call for the putting off, the abandonment of abuse, and then the putting on of righteousness. As we abandon our own way, we can embrace the peace that God has for us. Ultimately, the desired outcome of an intervention is to elicit a genuine response, whether that is one of repentance or rejection—either response brings clarity. This is a point that I make quite frequently when building teams. And this is the one that I think some of our churches are unaware of or don't think they need to broaden their worldview on. I frequently bring up to teams I participate in that *the outcome of this work is to determine where this person's heart is.*

If there is repentance, then the next phase is the work of discipleship. This discipleship should include meeting with an accountability group or a mentor, praying, and growing in areas of needed spiritual maturity such as kindness and gentleness for instance. Churches should be thoroughly equipped to walk out the process of growing in righteousness and conformity in Christ. These men, like all of us, need to depend on God for the strength to live as he has designed.

If the individual rejects our help, or continues to pursue their own agenda, or maintains aspects of control, then that brings insight as well. Many of us have been taught to ask ourselves, *Do I even have a counselee?* If he remains obstinate or hostile, then we have options for serving the victim, the church, and the unrepentant sinner, including completing the church discipline process. Remember, this is not simply about getting back to normal. In fact, it should be higher than normal. It should be getting to a place of greater maturity through discipleship. We're confronting sinners with the goal of creating mature believers so that they can confront sin in their own heart and life.

The Good Work of a Biblical Intervention

Many years ago, a faithful brother gave me some of the most useful advice I have ever received in ministry. He wasn't a pastor or a conference speaker or a well-known author. No, he was a deacon in a local church who had faithfully worked as a handyman for many years. He took the opportunity at a graduation party to look me in the eyes and say, "The best advice I can give you is to do your work well." That simple phrase has resonated with me over the years and rings true as we reflect on conducting interventions with those who have harmed their partners. Paul tells the Galatian Christians that good work is work worth doing, despite its sometimes tiring nature and burdensome weight. We are called to do good, and the work of intervening in domestic abuse situations is certainly good work.

CHAPTER 8

. . . .

Understanding the Mind and Heart of an Abusive Person

Greg Wilson

You don't have to look far to find information that purports to explain the nature of abusive individuals. Podcasts, online videos, popular books, and blogs abound that proclaim a definitive profile of abusers: they are narcissists or sociopaths (or they have another personality disorder), their anger is out of control, their substance abuse is to blame, etc. In reality, individuals who abuse do not fit neatly into such reductionist categories. However, with time and experience, certain characteristics, behaviors, and motivations emerge that give us a glimpse into the inner world of an abusive person.

Let's begin with the definition of abuse I use when counseling abusive individuals. It is *the desecration of the image of God through patterns of intentionally misusing power—covertly or overtly, in words or actions—to gratify self.* This definition starts with the *image of God.* In an abusive relationship, just as in any relationship, both people are image-bearers of God. Further, if they are believers, they are children of God. This is where we have to start. What makes abuse so horrific is that it desecrates the very essence of the unique role God gave humans—to reflect his character and goodness, to "image him," throughout the earth. Abuse happens when one image-bearer degrades another image-bearer through cruel or unjust treatment—the exact opposite of how God treats people. This is a double desecration: the image-bearing capacity of the abuser profaned, even as he defiles the image-bearing capacity of another.

Needless to say, each of us acts in ungodly ways, and none of us consistently reflect the character of God to one another. However, in abuse, there tend to be *patterns* of destructive, harmful, degrading, or harsh behavior. Clearly, many forms of physical and sexual abuse do not require the presence of multiple occurrences in order to label the conduct as abusive. However, in such cases, it is almost always true that a pattern of less-conspicuous-but-just-as-devastating verbal, emotional, psychological, spiritual, or financial abuse has previously existed, sometimes for years.

There is also *intentionality.* Intentionality can be confusing because often a counselee will say "I didn't mean to do that" or "I wasn't intending to do that." However, as a clinician with a biblical worldview/anthropology, I would reply that the Scriptures are quite clear that we don't always know and understand the intentions of our heart, and the intentions of our heart are frequently deceitful and wicked, as Jeremiah 17:9 says. I believe that abuse is always intentional, but the intention may not be initially obvious. Often, it shows up more intuitively—a learned or acquired behavior pattern that he has found will help him gain what he wants. An abusive person usually doesn't wake up in the morning and decide to gaslight his spouse just for fun. Instead, he may have learned that rolling his eyes in disbelief or calling his spouse forgetful or crazy is a means to his end. It is important for the counselor and both people in the relationship to understand that there is an (often hidden) intention behind what is happening, and we may need to work a bit to find that intention because our hearts tend to lie to us to cover up our sin.

While much of my definition thus far could describe other forms of sin, a key characteristic of abuse is that it always entails the misuse of power. In *Why Does He Do That?*, Lundy Bancroft states that "the defining point of abuse is when the man starts to exercise power over the woman in a way that causes harm to her and creates a privileged status for him." Abuse is only possible where power imbalances exist in relationships.[1] It isn't the imbalance of power that defines the relationship as abusive, however. That is simply the necessary precondition. It is the misuse of that power that leads to abuse. Pastors and elders sometimes spiritually abuse their parishioners. Parents sometimes abuse their children. Employers sometimes abuse their employees. In all these cases, those who occupy a position of power, authority, or influence have used it selfishly, to serve themselves. Instead of helping those under their influence to flourish by building them up, they have caused harm.

Power can be misused in both *overt and covert* ways: physical intimidation, threats, screaming, throwing things, demeaning words, as well as more subtle forms such as mind games, twisting words, sarcasm, manipulation, rewriting history, or playing the victim. Furthermore, abuse may be perpetrated in *words or actions*, e.g., words intended to tear down the other's confidence or sense of self or actions like monitoring a phone or restricting another's friendships. Regardless of the method used, ultimately abuse is about getting what I want or *gratifying self* in some way.

Other definitions of abuse abound, but most include these same basic concepts. The US Department of Justice defines "domestic violence" this way:

> We define domestic violence as a pattern of abusive behavior in any relationship that is used by one partner to gain or maintain power and control over another intimate partner. Domestic violence can be physical, sexual, emotional, economic, or psychological actions or threats of actions that influence another person. This includes any behaviors that intimidate, manipulate, humiliate, isolate, frighten, terrorize, coerce, threaten, blame, hurt, injure, or wound someone.[2]

1. Lundy Bancroft, *Why Does He Do That? Inside the Minds of Angry and Controlling Men* (New York: G. P. Putnam's Sons, 2002), 123–24.

2. United States Department of Justice, "What Is Domestic Violence," accessed February 6, 2023, https://www.justice.gov/ovw/domestic-violence.

In their book *Is It My Fault? Hope and Healing for Those Suffering Domestic Violence,* Justin and Lindsey Holcomb define it similarly:

> Domestic violence is a pattern of coercive, controlling, or abusive behavior that is used by one individual to gain or maintain power and control over another individual in the context of an intimate relationship. This includes any behaviors that retighten, intimidate, terrorize, exploit, manipulate, hurt, humiliate, blame, injure, or wound an intimate partner.[3]

Jeremy Pierre and I use a slightly different definition of abuse in our book, *When Home Hurts*: "Abuse occurs as a person in a position of greater influence uses his personal capacities to diminish the personal capacities of those under his influence in order to control them."[4] You can see in these definitions similar concepts of patterns of control, an imbalance of power (or influence) in the relationship, which is misused with the goal of using another person to gain what one wants for selfish intent. Each of these elements must be successfully addressed in the heart of the abuser in order to arrest his abusive behavior.

Broken Image-Bearers

I hope the descriptions above make it clear that abuse is abhorrent. So what kind of person would perpetrate such evil? This is why the first phrase in my definition above, "a desecration of the image of God" is so important. Every abusive person is, first and foremost, a *person* created in the image of God. This person is someone's partner or husband or friend. He's not a monster or villain, but a human being, created in the image of God to bear his likeness. In our work with abusive men, Chris Moles and I use similar language—we try to be winsome, to get to know the flawed person behind the behavior. To be curious

3. Justin S. Holcomb and Lindsey A. Holcomb, *Is It My Fault? Hope and Healing for Those Suffering Domestic Violence* (Chicago: Moody, 2014), 57.

4. Jeremy Pierre and Greg Wilson, *When Home Hurts: A Guide for Wisely Responding to Domestic Abuse in Your Church* (Fearn, Scotland: Christian Focus, 2021), 39.

about him. Even to enjoy getting to know him. That's where we start. That is where all counseling starts because every human receiving your counsel and care is broken. Specifically, he is broken from three distinct root causes: because the whole world is broken, because of the results of others' sins against him, and because of his own sin.

There are a number of ways in which the person in front of you may demonstrate the effects of living in a fallen world. As a clinician, I'm aware that this person may suffer from a diagnosable disorder of body or soul. He may be clinically depressed. He may suffer from anxiety. He may have a disorder that affects executive functioning in the brain, such as obsessive–compulsive disorder, attention deficit hyperactivity disorder, or autism spectrum disorder. He may have experienced a traumatic event (or events) and have a PTSD diagnosis. Or, as mentioned above, he may actually have a personality disorder, though the prevalence of diagnosable personality disorders is much lower than what most popular media might indicate. The usual culprits consistent with abusive behavior patterns are narcissistic personality disorder, borderline personality disorder, antisocial personality disorder, or schizotypal personality disorder, although other personality disorders have been implicated as well. Any of the above conditions may sometimes elucidate or contribute to some of the behaviors that show up in abuse, but none of them are causal.

The abusive person may also have been socialized into unhealthy patterns of relating to others. Unhelpful or untrue ways of thinking about God, others, or ourselves can also lead us to behave in thoughtless or uncaring ways. Shame, fear, anger, and other unbridled negative emotions can also play a part. We all live as broken people in a broken world and suffer as a result. If we don't recognize how our suffering is affecting us and find healing, our suffering will inevitably spill out onto others.

Another way that our suffering can impact abusive behavior is when we are broken because of the sins others have committed against us. As I am getting to know the abusive person in front of me,

I view them through what I would call a trauma-informed lens. This simply means that I recognize that many people hurt others because they have been hurt. You could say that they have learned to deal with their own past hurts in an unhealthy way—by hurting others.

In my practice with abusive people, I have found that abandonment and abuse are the most common past hurts that arise. Perhaps they may carry hurt from having been abandoned by a parent or caregiver due to divorce or some other relational break. They may have experienced abuse in the past either as the primary victim (the abuse was directed toward them) or as a secondary victim (they are part of the collateral damage that occurred when one of their parents was abusive toward the other, for example). In this case, they may just be repeating a learned pattern of behavior from their own childhood. But they also may try to work through unresolved trauma from a previous time of life in unhealthy ways. Again, this is not an excuse for abusive actions. But understanding and exploring these wounds can help us address the root of their power and control issues later on.

So, like all of us, every abusive person is broken because they were born into a sinful world and have experienced the sins of others against them. Of course, there is one more way that human brokenness affects all of us—we sin against others. But the sin of abuse, as we have defined it as a double desecration of the image of God, is different from other relational sins in some fundamental and particular ways.

Abuse versus Other Relational Sins

Abuse is definitely sin, but it differs in kind and degree from other relational sins. In some ways, we all "abuse" each other on a daily basis, especially in our closest relationships. In our book, *When Home Hurts*, Jeremy Pierre and I differentiate between abuse and other relational sins using analogous relationships found in nature. In the natural world, relationships between and within species can be competitive, parasitic, or predatory. We speak about normal, typical "relational sins" as competitive. The people in the relationship pit themselves against each other because they both want to win in some way. In marriage counseling, I'll often ask a couple, "What does a typical fight look like?" The response often is one of embarrassment because a fight started off with something very small and seemingly insignificant. Mexican versus Italian food for dinner, beach or mountain areas for vacation, or spending or saving for something. In these conflicts, each person is convinced that they are right or deserving and competes with the other for their own way. Neither wants to give in to the other. This, by itself, is not abuse, but rather typical, sinful marital conflict.

Abuse, on the other hand, moves past competition and becomes parasitic or predatory in nature. A predator goes after someone or something else that is weaker, and they have some kind of advantage: size, cunning, speed, etc. Then they use that advantage to get what they want, damaging the victim in the process. That's what a predator does. A parasite, on the other hand, latches on to someone and sucks the life out of them in a more covert way.

One way of thinking about abuse relative to other relational sin is to say that most relational sin is competitive, while abuse is parasitic or predatory. In competition, each person is saying "Me before you" and "I'm more important to me than you are right now. Not all the time, just right now. My preference of Mexican food is more important than yours for Italian. So I'm not considering you; I'm putting myself before you." This is common in all of our relationships; each of us is selfish at heart and we want our own way. The object is to "win," not to diminish or control the other person. This is typical relational sin. In contrast, sin that is abusive is "me *over* you." It is predatory or parasitic. It makes the other person smaller or weaker in some way, reducing their capacity to act or to grow or to see reality. The harm caused by a predator is more direct, overt, and explicit; the harm caused by a parasite is more indirect, covert, and subtle in its diminishing effect. However, both are abusive, and both are about me using my influence to diminish the personal capacity, the agency, the will of another in the relationship, and controlling them to get what I want.

These distinctions may seem arbitrary or confusing, but they become clearer as you work in these situations. Judith Herman, in her seminal work, *Trauma and Recovery*, describes some of the ways that abusive people operate within relationships. As you read her description of abusive patterns, you can sense a difference between the conflict of two people who have basic regard for one another but are sinful and selfish, and the dark heart of abuse. Again, we don't want to view perpetrators of abuse as monsters or villains, but we must tell the truth about what is happening. Here is how Judith Herman describes it:

> In order to escape accountability for his crimes, the perpetrator does everything in his power to promote forgetting. Secrecy and silence are the perpetrator's first line of defense. If secrecy fails, the perpetrator attacks the credibility of his victim. If he cannot silence her absolutely, he tries to make sure that no one listens. To this end, he marshals an impressive array of arguments, from the most blatant denial to the most sophisticated and elegant rationalization. After every atrocity one can expect to hear the same predictable apologies: it never happened, the victim lies, the victim exaggerates, the victim brought it upon herself; and in any case it is time to forget the past and move on. The more powerful the perpetrator, the greater is his prerogative to name and define reality, and the more completely his arguments prevail.[5]

You can see the elements of power and control in Herman's description. The language she uses connotes the predatorial and intentional nature of abuse.

5. Judith Herman, M.D., *Trauma and Recovery: The Aftermath of Violence—From Domestic Abuse to Political Terror* (New York: Basic Books, 1992), 8.

Abuse can also be differentiated from normal relational sin in terms of degree of impact, and in terms of persistence—how long it goes on. Abuse denigrates, decimates, and demeans the other person—it tears down their personal capacities of agency, decision-making, will, comprehension of reality, understanding of God, and ability to represent God to others. Victims are traumatized; they are overwhelmed by the abuser's array of physical and/or emotional tactics to the point that they can no longer respond effectively. Furthermore, abuse takes place over time—instances of severe physical abuse don't spring up out of thin air. Abusive patterns develop over time and typically increase in severity. When working with an abuser, I often hear that a certain behavior—name-calling, for instance—happens occasionally. However, when speaking to the victim, I learn that this has been happening consistently over the years with the names and adjectives worsening.

Hopefully you can begin to see how abuse is different from typical relational conflict, both in kind and degree. This is why we don't do marriage counseling when there's abuse—we're not dealing with typical marriage conflict. The dynamics, the landscape, the emotional infrastructure of the relationship, are completely different. We must help the victim begin to see herself rightly and rebuild, by the Spirit, what the abuser has torn down, and we must help the abuser see himself and his actions as a desecration, both of himself and his spouse, of what God has deemed holy and sacred.

Corrupt Perceptions Lead to Corrupt Behaviors

With all of these things in mind, here is a working definition of an abusive person: "An abusive person is an image-bearer of God, whose perceptions of God and himself are corrupted in particularly devastating ways, leading to corrupt ways of behaving."[6] This definition focuses on corrupted perceptions that lead to corrupt behavior. When attempting to help an abusive person, you must realize that his

6. Pierre and Wilson, *When Home Hurts*, 47.

perceptions of God, himself, and others are terribly corrupted, which leads him to act in corrupt and harmful ways.

So what are those corrupted perceptions? First, it must be acknowledged that having corrupted perceptions means that an abusive person does not see rightly. Perhaps this way of seeing life stems from their past hurts, or from their false beliefs, or from shame they feel—any number of factors could be contributing. And these corrupted ways of seeing exist on three levels: self, others, and God. When an abusive person sees himself, he doesn't see the reality of who he is or what he's doing. He always sees himself as better than he actually is. For example, he may be extremely focused on the house being clean when he gets home and critical of his spouse's inability to keep things to his standard. But he would say of himself that he's not nitpicking—he's simply precise. He's just stating an objective fact that the home is not "clean" (according to his definition of clean). In another example, he may see himself as "strong and decisive," whereas his family members experience him as demanding and tyrannical.

Unfortunately, in our world and in our churches, masculinity is often defined and expressed in un-Christlike ways. Positive qualities such as strength, leadership, action, and decisiveness are taken to ungodly extremes, often supported by a subtle belief in male superiority and entitlement. Similarly, an abusive person may view himself as "tough," which he considers a good and "manly" quality, whereas in reality he is cruel and brutal, without compassion or empathy for others. Such perceptions of self as strong, decisive, precise, honest, and tough give sanction to the abusive person to pursue his desires through abusive actions. This doesn't always happen for him on a conscious level. Often, we have to gently draw out this underlying motivation of self-gratification through curiosity and good questions. But it is always there. In his teaching seminars, Chris Moles often calls this type of curious inquiry "pulling the rope," and it's an important aspect of our work with abusers.

An abusive person may not be able to see others clearly either. He may objectify them—seeing them only as a means to getting what he wants or an obstacle in his way. He may lack social awareness or emotional intelligence, which leads him to regularly misperceive or misinterpret the words and actions of others. This inability to relate well to others or to treat them as objects often makes it difficult for him to listen to others or have compassion and empathy for them.

Lastly, God is often nonexistent or irrelevant to the abuser's heart and motives. They may profess faith, be active in a church, or even be well-respected for their theological acumen, but beneath this external faith, love of God is not a motivation or compelling influence. Worse, God is often used as the justifying authority for his controlling actions. Refrains such as "You submit; God has called me to be the head" or "God made me the leader of this household" are wielded over family members like a bludgeoning hammer, again allowing the abuser to carry on with whatever plans he deems best for himself.

A Closer Look Inside the Heart

The diagram[7] on the next page illustrates several perceptions and behaviors common to abusive people. You'll notice that the "power/control" circle is larger than the others, as is the "entitlement" circle. This is intentional and designed to emphasize that entitlement is the most prevalent perception among abusers, while wielding power and control is most prominent among their behaviors. Not only are these perceptions and behaviors prevalent, they are also primary. The other circles are factors, and they're important, but entitlement is key among the perceptions. An abusive person is motivated by a core belief that he deserves to get what he wants, over and above what is good or best for anyone else. Deconstruction of this core belief is essential in our work with abusers.

7. Adapted from Pierre and Wilson, *When Home Hurts,* 174. Used by permission.

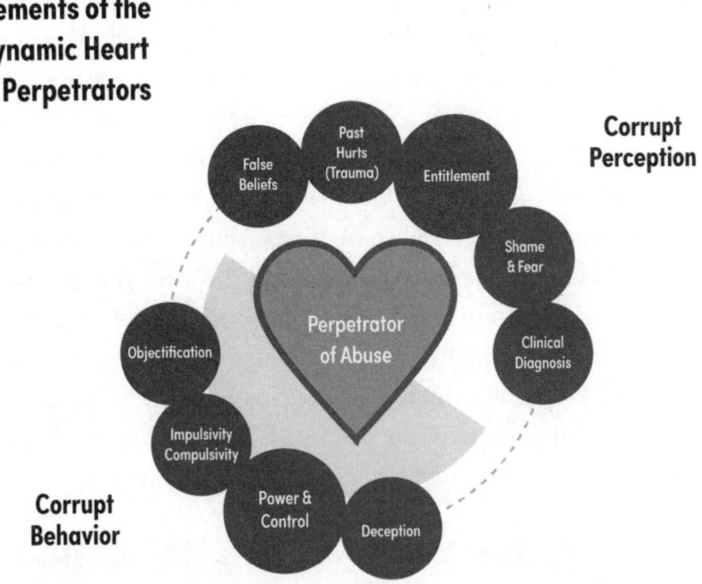

False beliefs about God, himself, or others, also support or encourage corrupt behaviors in abusive people. False beliefs may include thoughts like "all women should submit to men," "a wife is an extension of her husband," "as long as we are married, I can treat you however I want to," "the husband gets the final say in all important decisions," or "as a man, I'm better able to interpret Scripture."

Additionally, the past traumas that abusers have undergone may underlie much of their behavior. Abuse is often a generational pattern—many abusers were themselves abused. Abandonment, grief, experiences of or witnessing violence—each of these can significantly color the way an abuser views himself, others, and God. Often, we see feelings of shame at the root of abusive behavior. Lastly, as mentioned earlier, biopsychosocial factors such as ADHD, OCD, PTSD, physical or intellectual disabilities and the like may impact how an abusive person sees his reality and the ways he attempts to gain control over his world. It's easy to see how each of these areas overlap and influence one another. Many perceptions may fall into more than one category, and perceptions in one category impact or undergird perceptions in another. However, these are just a handful of misperceptions that we typically find at the root of an abusive person's actions.

Now we turn our attention to abusive behaviors. Here we see the "power and control" circle as key. The primary belief of entitlement, fueled by other false beliefs, past hurts, shame, or biopsychosocial factors, underlie the primary acts of control and domination that characterize abuse. In his book *The Batterer as Parent*, Lundy Bancroft states, "The overarching behavioral characteristic of the batterer is the imposition of a pattern of control over his partner."[8] This exercise of coercive control can show up in almost any area of a relationship. As I mentioned earlier, it may be reflected in more overt ways such as physical or sexual assault, blocking doorways to prevent movement, slamming doors, throwing objects, yelling, or name-calling. Or it may be demonstrated in more subversive or covert behaviors like manipulating, using the children, isolating, controlling finances, displaying weapons, playing mind games, minimizing, denying, and blaming. Each abusive person may exhibit a different profile of behaviors, but almost all of those behaviors support the idea "I am in control." Furthermore, it is well understood that, over time, the abuser's need for control expands, and his grip strengthens. It's important to understand this at the outset: abusive behavior is a symptom of a much bigger problem, and, if untreated, will worsen. There is no such thing as an abuser who starts off with intimidation and just stays there. The cancer is most definitely malignant and aggressive, wreaking more and more havoc in the family.

Objectification of others, particularly of a spouse, is another behavior common in abusive people. Andrew Bauman has written about the problem of objectification related to pornographic addictions. He talks about a "pornographic style of relating," which allows

8. Lundy Bancroft, Jay G. Silverman, and Daniel Ritchie, *The Batterer as Parent: Addressing the Impact of Domestic Violence on Family Dynamics*, 2nd ed. (Thousand Oaks, CA: Sage Publications, 2012), 6.

us to see that objectification is not just a behavior, but is a way of relating to the world.[9] An abusive person frequently objectifies women by seeing them as a means to his gratification, sexual or otherwise. In truth, he relates to everyone around him in terms of how they can give him what he wants—acceptance, approval, membership, sex, accolades, etc. It may become the job of the family to make him look good in public, and failure to do so may result in punishment, shaming, yelling, or isolation.

In my work with abusive men, I frequently see the characteristics of impulsivity or compulsivity and risk-taking. These are characteristics common to addicts, and there is definitely some overlap between abusive and addictive behavior. An abusive person is so desperate to get what he wants that he may take risks or act impulsively, similar to an addict. It is also not unusual, in my experience, for abusive people to also struggle with addictions (pornography, gambling, chemical addiction, sex addiction). Furthermore, I have found that executive functioning issues (as with ADHD, OCD, and Autism Spectrum Disorder) often lead to impulsivity, which also impact the behavior of the abuser. This is not to say that any specific percentage of abusive people struggle with ADHD, OCD, or autism, but it is important to be aware that these disorders can coexist with and exacerbate abusive behaviors.

Finally, deception is a common *modus operandi* of abusers. They can be shady, rarely telling you any more than they are pretty sure you already know. They hide their addictions and abusive actions, lie about them, and deceive others to put themselves in the best light. They gaslight their spouse, calling her uninformed or naive or stupid or crazy. They are also almost always self-deceived. They lack awareness of many of the corrupt perceptions and behaviors that I have discussed above. An abusive person would likely read this chapter and not see himself in it at all. Meanwhile his victim would clearly see him in some of the descriptions above and find it shocking that he (and

9. Andrew J. Bauman, *The Psychology of Porn: Essays on Pornography, Objectification, and Healing* (Self-published, 2018), 16–20.

others who think they know him) can't see it. If an abuser is going to make progress, these are the areas of his behavior—use of power to control, objectification, impulsivity and risk-taking, and deceit—that will need to be worked on in depth in counseling.

The abusive person is a person broken in all the ways that you and I are, but also corrupted by ways of seeing others and ways of behaving in the world that lead to particularly devastating relational consequences. If we are to care well for families caught up in the chaos of domestic abuse, we must be able to see the abusive person fully and rightly and help him see himself fully and rightly. If he does, there is a better chance that he will turn from his abusive behaviors and lead a life marked by humility, grace, and peace. And it is far more likely that those in close relationship with him will experience flourishing rather than destruction.

CHAPTER 9

....

Counseling the Abusive Individual

Greg Wilson

In the previous chapter, my aim was to present a biblical picture of the dynamic heart of an individual who acts in ways that are destructive in his closest relationships. My hope as we consider how to counsel and care is that we would not caricaturize or villainize the people we are trying to help. People who behave in abusive and destructive ways behind closed doors usually look like your next-door neighbor, the person who bought you coffee this morning, someone who is in your church small group, or even your best friend. In fact, any of those people *could* be the person I was describing in the last chapter. My burden in this chapter is to describe how to best care for such a person in a way that they might change and be marked by peace and the fruit of the Spirit instead of violence and oppression.

Historically, secular batterer intervention prevention programs (BIPP) groups have done most of the heavy lifting in working with people who have exhibited abusive behaviors. And these classes have been helpful. Led by trained facilitators, they are typically accessible to almost everyone. Sometimes they only admit people who have been referred to them from the criminal justice system, usually as a part of a deferred adjudication program. But other programs will admit voluntary participants. The word *batterer* in the name might give you pause, especially when you hear that many of them only draw participants from the criminal justice system. But it shouldn't. Practitioners in the field often use the terms *abuser*, *perpetrator*, and *batterer* synonymously—just as the terms *domestic abuse* and *domestic violence* are used synonymously. From a biblical perspective, it is important to remember that other types of abuse besides sexual abuse and physical abuse (such as emotional, psychological, financial/economic, verbal, and spiritual abuse) are no less "violent." Remember James's description of verbal abuse.

The tongue, James says, is "a fire, a world of unrighteousness." It stains "the whole body, setting on fire the entire course of life, and set on fire by hell." It is "a restless evil, full of deadly poison. With it we bless our Lord and Father, and with it we curse people who are made in the likeness of God" (James 3:6–9). That's a very violent picture, and as far as I can tell, the perpetrator described here didn't lay a hand on anyone. Jesus describes the sin of murder as something that has already been conceived in a person's heart when they slander and insult a fellow image-bearer (Matthew 5:21–22). And James again makes essentially the same claim when he refers to murder as the ultimate outcome of fights and quarrels (James 4:1–2). The person engaged in caring for the perpetrator needs to understand his abusive behavior as a violent desecration of the image of God, as I described in the last chapter, regardless of the precise nature of the behavior.

Chris Moles gained his initial experience working with abusive men as a trained batterer interventionist, leading BIPP groups in West Virginia, while also serving as a biblical counselor and pastor. I write from the perspective of a licensed professional counselor (LPC) who also identifies as a biblical counselor, a care deacon at my church, and a former pastor. Though I have facilitated education and accountability groups for abusive individuals, most of my work in this space has come in the counseling office, sitting with men whose behavior has been identified as abusive. While Chris and I both recommend education/accountability groups, such as BIPP, Men of Peace,[1] and

1. Men of Peace groups are education and accountability groups that use a biblical framework to help destructive individuals become more peaceful and Christlike in their relationships. For more information, visit menofpeace.org.

G-5[2] groups, as well as individual counseling for perpetrators of abuse, this chapter is for *anyone* who is in the position of caring for such a person. We hope that professional counselors and those who care for abusive individuals in other contexts will read this book. But we know that most of our readers want to know how best to care for abusive individuals in the local church context. Your care will be most effective as you leverage the training and experience of seasoned practitioners.

Ed Gondolf has done the most research on the effectiveness of various approaches to intervention with perpetrators. Gondolf's verdict is that the various approaches that he studied "show promise, but warrant improvement."[3] While Etiony Aldarondo, another researcher, states that his data demonstrates "that each level of intervention is making modest and important contributions to stop and reduce violent behavior,"[4] Chris Murphy and Laura Ting report that their research suggests that "valid debates remain."[5] Many in the field would concur that change is uncertain and often incremental. However, if just one entitled attitude is acknowledged and owned, or one small but harmful behavior is stopped, life will improve for both the abuser and his family. Even if the couple divorces, there will most likely still be some level of future relationship and interaction, especially if there are children involved. Even incremental improvement means less suffering for all involved.

In the body of Christ, we have a resource that many of these practitioners lack—the Holy Spirit, who can make hearts of stone become hearts of flesh. If Saul, the chief of sinners, can become Paul, the apostle to the Gentiles, then even the vilest abuser can be saved and

2. G-5 men's groups, based on Galatians 5:22–23, are education and accountability groups for men who use power and control in relationships and are committed to working toward lasting change. For more information, visit https://www.calledtopeace.org/g5men/.

3. Edward W. Gondolf, *The Future of Batterer Programs: Reassessing Evidence-Based Practice* (Boston: Northeastern University Press, 2012), 77.

4. Etiony Aldarondo, "Evaluating the Efficacy of Interventions with Men Who Batter," chapter 3 in E. Aldarondo and F. Mederos eds., *Programs for Men Who Batter: Intervention and Prevention Strategies in a Diverse Society* (Kingston, NJ: Civic Research Institute, 2002), 16.

5. Chris Murphy and Laura Ting, "Interventions for Perpetrators of Intimate Partner Violence: A Review of Efficacy Research and Recent Trends," *Partner Abuse* 1, no. 1 (2010): 1, 40.

changed. Of course, holding out hope for Spirit-fueled change does not mean that it is wise for an abuser's wife and children to remain with the abuser. But it does help us as counselors and pastors labor in hope and persevere in prayer.

Working with abusive people often feels a bit like the work of Jeremiah or Isaiah—you care in grace and truth as well as you can, but in the end there is a high likelihood that they will reject you and/or your message. It is hard work, and often the fruit, if there is any, is so far down the road that you may never see it. I don't recommend that anyone engage in this work alone, or exclusively. It is helpful for me as a counselor that I work with a variety of populations and issues. It is also advantageous that I do this work in the company of colleagues, including the other contributors to this volume. Care for a variety of people and situations and surround yourself with others who love Jesus and you.

Although many, if not most, abusive persons who show up for care will have ulterior or suspicious motives, the fact that an abusive person is willing to even meet with you is a testament to the image of God in him. And if he is willing to come, we will do our best, with the Spirit's help, to give some sight to blind eyes and help the lame to at least take a small step, for the glory of God and the benefit of the family.

The Most Important Rule of Engagement

Safety, for the spouse, children, and any others living with the abusive person, is always the highest priority in the church's care for the abusive individual. It is always recommended that a safety plan be in place for the victim and that the victim's advice and consent be obtained before you engage a perpetrator in *any* way. I use the constitutional terminology of "advice and consent" because it's concise and easy to remember. By *consent*, I mean that it should not come as a surprise to the victim that you are engaging her husband. Each time her husband is engaged in discussing ways that he has caused harm to his partner, you are creating a potentially unsafe situation for the spouse. You aren't coming home with him, and, even if the couple is separated, abusive retaliatory behavior can still occur. Only those who live in the home of an abuser can accurately gauge how he might retaliate or how safe they feel under various scenarios. Church leaders, if you are going to meet with an abusive partner to discuss his abusive behavior, please ask the permission of those who have been harmed by his behavior. By *advice,* I simply mean that you want to ask the victim for insight about the *what* and the *how* of this conversation before you have it: time and location of the meeting, personnel attending the meeting, topics to be discussed, etc. She has a right to know anything that might be discussed about her or her situation that impacts her safety (which could be anything) when meeting with the church.[6]

Let me give an example. You are a church care team member, staff member, home group leader, elder, or pastor, and a woman in your church has reported that she is experiencing abusive behavior from her husband. You know from her counselor and/or advocate (or from her directly) that a safety plan is in place. You are still going to wait to have a conversation with him until you know that she is ready for you to take this step (from her directly or from her counselor and/or advocate speaking for her) *and* that she has okayed everything you are planning to confront him on. Let's say that she reported the following behaviors to you: demeaning words, harsh and condescending tone, constant criticism, and once punching his fist through the wall in their bedroom. You are going to say, "Jane, we are planning on meeting with John today to discuss his behaviors of demeaning words, harsh and condescending tone, constant criticism, and the incident in which he punched the wall in your bedroom. Jane might say, "Thank

6. Some readers may be professional counselors or you may be hoping to collaborate with licensed professionals who are caring for either the victim or the perpetrator. State-licensed professionals, like me, usually operate within important professional codes and standards that require that we maintain our counselee's confidentiality, except in particular excepted circumstances (usually related to imminent life-threatening harm to self or others). When you are working with a professional counselor, it is very important that you respect the confidentiality of the professional relationship and request a release of information from the counselee before asking a professional counselor to collaborate with the team.

you for letting me know." Or she might say, "Oh dear, I forgot that I told you about the wall. I'm not ready for that to come out yet. Can you please not mention that incident right now?" If she responds in that way, your appropriate response is, "Thanks for letting us know. We will not bring up that incident until you are ready, but we will bring up the others. Is that okay?" The key is to bear in mind that each instance of "confrontation" or discussion about the harm that he is causing can potentially trigger a harsh and escalated response toward her—even if he appears fine when he leaves you. Therefore, it is also good to report to the victim (or her counselor/advocate) how the conversation went, what was said, and how he left the conversation after it ended.

If this sounds like a lot of work, well, it is. But it is also *care*—and that is what we are to do in this situation.

Counseling the Abuser

Once the victim's safety has been established and you have obtained her advice and consent, you can carefully begin working with the abuser. In a first meeting you should make clear that you take her experience of abuse very seriously and that you also want to hear any concerns that he has. You will want to clarify what Scripture says about abuse and how the church responds, based on your church's policy and protocol for responding to abuse.[7] It is also important to set clear expectations moving forward and help him develop a plan for personal accountability. The key elements of a personal accountability plan are shown in the box on the next page:

---

7. For more information on developing a robust policy and protocol for handling domestic abuse in your church, I recommend the following resources:

- Chris Moles, "Churches and Domestic Abuse Policy," blog post at chrismoles.org, October 14, 2018, http://www.chrismoles.org/news/2018/10/12/churches-and-domestic-abuse-policy,
- Greg Wilson, "Why Your Church Needs a Domestic Abuse Policy," blog post at chrismoles.org, December 3, 2017, http://www.chrismoles.org/news/2017/12/1/why-your-church-needs-a-domestic-abuse-policy,
- Jeremy Pierre and Greg Wilson, *When Home Hurts: A Guide for Responding Wisely to Domestic Abuse in Your Church* (Fearn, Scotland: Christian Focus Publications, 2021).

Key Elements of a Personal Accountability Plan

The Personal Accountability Plan contains the following elements:

- Discontinuing specific abusive behaviors once pointed out, with clear next steps if further abuse occurs.
- Accountability
  - To whom?
  - For what?
- Education/Accountability Group, such as BIPP or Men of Peace
- Individual counseling, with Release of Information (ROI) if possible
- Standards of care explained: how and to what extent will the church be involved in care moving forward?

This plan should have the goal of "no abuse." While it is certain that some abusive behaviors will continue while the abuser is beginning to see and own his abusive behavior, it is still important to set "no abuse" as the expectation. The perpetrator may object that you are requiring him to behave perfectly, but of course nothing could be further from the truth. The Scriptures are clear that no man except for Jesus was ever perfect. However, once a particular behavior has been named as destructive or abusive, it is a reasonable expectation for it to stop. You aren't requiring perfection—just that he behaves in non-abusive ways.

Then the plan must also clearly state what steps will be taken if further abuse occurs. In addition, the plan should detail who is holding him accountable and when/where they will be meeting. Accountability could be with church members, church staff, or others who have agreed to be in this role. But we recommend that at least one person in the accountability group has received some training in abuse issues or is part of a trained abuse response team in your church. Often, the abusive person is responsible for keeping some sort of "log" to record incidents of abuse. It should include details such as "this is what happened," "this is what I wanted," and "this is how my spouse responded." It's also helpful to include space to imagine a different scenario: "this is how I could have responded better" or "this is what might have happened if I had responded differently." The incidents and his reflections on them can be discussed with his accountability partners, with a batterer intervention, Men of Peace, G-5 group, or with a counselor.

Self-Reflection Log (to be completed after each incident of destructive behavior)

What Happened?

1. What did you do? (Name specific behaviors.)
2. What did you want or fear losing?
3. How does this behavior reveal your functional view of God, your wife, or yourself?
4. What was the impact of your behavior?

Questions to Help You Seek the Lord in This Situation:

1. How does God view this behavior?
2. What does it look like to turn to him in this situation?

How God Wants You to Respond in the Future:

1. What does a God-trusting response look like?
2. What would be the impact of this new God-trusting behavior?

Both individual counseling and education/accountability through some kind of group format are essential to helping an abusive person change. In many cases, a church may not be involved or may be ill-equipped to handle situations of abuse. Does the church have standards of care for handling situations of abuse? Does it have anyone who has received training in working in this area? A church's involvement will vary, depending on its resources and experience. Regardless of the level of involvement, it is important to spell out what is expected of each person involved with the family: counselor, advocate (if applicable), accountability group members, and pastor (if applicable). With clear guidelines and good communication, a team can be a huge help in the process of healing from abuse, for both the victim and the abuser.

Assessing for Risk and Openness to Change

It is important for those working with an abusive person to make some assessment regarding the level of danger that he presents and his openness to change. Whether you are a professional counselor or a church care ministry, there is some level of risk that you should not be willing to accept, and there needs to be some level of openness to change that it is reasonable to expect. A simple way to conceptualize risk and openness to change is a continuum with three basic reference levels based upon the abuser's response to your engagement of him: "hostile," "reluctant or resistant" (sometimes called "ambivalent"), and "open," as shown in the diagram below.

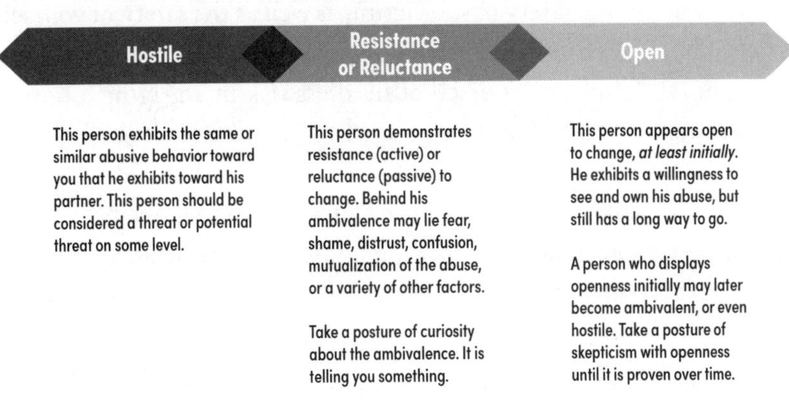

This conceptualization is only intended to be a generalized and informal way of describing the types of responses that you may initially receive, not as a definitive categorization of abuser risk. If there is any doubt about risk, it is always a good idea to have a formal risk assessment conducted by a professional trained in one of several available risk assessment instruments.[8] We urge you to take the assessment of perpetrator dangerousness extremely seriously.

Some men will respond to your efforts to point out concerns about their destructive behavior by exhibiting the same or similar behavior toward you they use with their partner—anger, hostility, or aggression. Or his response may be just the opposite—calm, reasonable, even apologetic—until he gets home. This is where abuser intervention can become confusing and difficult. When in doubt, you should trust his victim's assessment of him more than your own.

A **hostile** response, whether it occurs in your presence or is reported by his victim, should be concerning. His risk level is high and his openness to change is usually very low. We would recommend that you refer a hostile person to a batterer intervention program (BIPP), at least as a first step. Almost every county has one, and the leaders of such groups are trained in how to engage a more aggressive perpetrator population. If the criminal justice system has been involved, a court will often mandate a BIPP. In these instances, you must think carefully about the safety of the victim, as well as the safety of yourself or any church staff/members who are involved. Don't put the victim, your church family, or yourself at needless risk in engaging a hostile perpetrator. Churches are ill-equipped to handle hostile, belligerent, or aggressive perpetrators.

The most likely initial response from a person who is being confronted with concern about his potentially abusive behavior is some level of **ambivalence**, which is often characterized by reluctance (its

---

8. A professional can conduct a formal risk assessment of the likelihood of a perpetrator to reassault. Professionals often use an intimate partner violence prediction instrument such as

- Danger Assessment Instrument (Jacquelyn C. Campbell and Jill Theresa Messing, *Assessing Dangerousness, Third Edition: Domestic Violence Offenders and Child Abusers* (Thousand Oaks, CA: Sage, 1995)
- Spousal Assault Risk Assessment Guide (Philip Randall Kropp, *Manual for the Spousal Assault Risk Assessment Guide* [Vancouver, BC: British Columbia Institute Against Family Violence, 1995])
- Partner Assault Prognostic Scale (Christopher M. Murphy, "A Prognostic Indicator Scale for the Treatment of Domestic Abuse Perpetrators," *Journal of Interpersonal Violence* 18: 1087–105)
- The Mosaic Assessment (mosaicmethod.com).

passive form) or resistance (the active form). Reluctance or resistance to change in an abusive person is something you can work with. This person is not abusive in his response to you—he just may not agree with your assessment of his behavior and may not seem to care much about changing. A person who shows reluctance or resistance may simply be convinced that you are wrong. He may believe that once you hear his side of the story, you will change your mind and understand why he is justified in his actions. He may minimize, deny, justify, or blame the victim in response to specific examples of potentially abusive behavior, but not in a way that demonstrates overt aggression. In the language of motivational interviewing, we encourage you to roll with reluctance and resistance.[9] Show curiosity and ask questions to attempt to uncover what's going on in the abuser's mind—what's underneath his ambivalence to change. For example, is he distrustful of the person trying to give care (pastor, counselor, etc.)? Or is shame or fear—perhaps fear of vulnerability or change—at the root of his reluctance. Resistance to change should be reframed from "he is just not cooperative," which is an unhelpful perspective that will lead nowhere even if true. More helpfully, consider that he might misunderstand the problem or not want your care.

While some abusers are hostile and others are reluctant or resistant, a few will come giving at least the appearance of being **open** to change. As they move through the process, they may regress into a position of ambivalence or hostility, but at least initially they are willing to consider the idea that they may have destructive patterns in the ways that they relate to others. They reflect a willingness to talk

9. William R. Miller and Stephen Rollnick, *Motivational Interviewing: Helping People Change*, 3rd ed. (New York: Guilford Press, 2013), 12. At its simplest level, motivational interviewing is "a collaborative conversation style for strengthening a person's own motivation and commitment to change." To read more on how motivational interviewing can be applied to work with perpetrators of domestic abuse to enhance motivation to change, we recommend Christopher M. Murphy and Christopher I. Eckhardt, "Enhancing Motivation to Change and Engagement into Treatment," chapter 7 in *Treating the Abusive Partner: An Individualized Cognitive-Behavioral Approach* (New York: Guilford Press, 2005), 135–66. A book-length treatment with research and data can be found in Christopher Murphy and Roland D. Maiuro, eds., *Motivational Interviewing and Stages of Change in Intimate Partner Violence* (New York: Springer, 2009).

about it and see whether or not there's something there. We should also be aware that the way a person presents to us in the first couple of meetings may not be who they really are. They may present as open, but when you start digging deeper, they become resistant or hostile. Or they may present as resistant and then move toward more openness. Regardless, it's important to assess in your mind where the person is on the continuum so that you can provide the appropriate level of care.

The Importance of Communication and Consistency

Throughout the counseling process, it is important to keep communication flowing between the various supporting members of a couple's care team. For instance, after meeting with the victim and her advocate, you may become aware of some new or additional safety issues for the victim. You may need to revise her safety plan after hearing a new concern that she has. You also may need to make appropriate referrals to professionals or groups.

Following through and following up are really important in this work as well. If the abusive person has any underlying conditions such as OCD, ADHD, or Autism Spectrum Disorder, maintaining a tight and consistent structure for accountability and counseling will be essential for his progress. In such cases, you should keep any mental health professionals in the loop, in whatever way that is appropriate through the use of releases of information (ROIs) with the professional, if possible, or just by asking if he is following up with his own health and care. Otherwise if an abuser is looking for a reason to disregard what you or his spouse is asking him to do, which is often the case, any underlying condition may give him an excuse for failing to show up for accountability meetings or failing to check in regularly and consistently. This, in turn, may be just the excuse he wants to quit the process altogether. We want to equip ourselves and those who are walking alongside abusers to be consistent and communicate well as we hope and labor for the best possible outcomes.

The Path to Progress

Of course, the best possible outcome of this work is repentance—true heart change leading to different, peaceful, righteous, non-abusive behaviors. In 2 Corinthians 7:9–13, Paul describes a type of grief that is not consistent with repentance, which he calls worldly grief leading to death. In this same text, he also describes a type of grief that is consistent with repentance, which he calls godly grief leading to salvation without regret. In this text, Paul helpfully names for the Corinthians some of their observable behaviors that demonstrated to him that their repentance was genuine. Genuine repentance takes time to discern because it involves observing changed behavior that is consistently demonstrated over time.

In *When Home Hurts*, Jeremy Pierre and I assert that repentance involves **seeing** and naming your sin accurately, **owning** it (without avoiding accountability by minimizing, denying, and blaming the victim), **hating** the sin increasingly because God hates it and because it separates us from him, and, ultimately, **turning** from the sin through time-tested changes in behavior.[10] The diagram on the next page is an attempt to name some behavioral markers that can demonstrate that the abusive person is seeing, owning, hating, and turning from his sin. It illustrates a pathway of progress that we hope to see an abusive person begin to take on his journey of repentance.

10. Pierre and Wilson, *When Home Hurts*. Pages 189–209 give detail on this understanding of repentance in abusive situations.

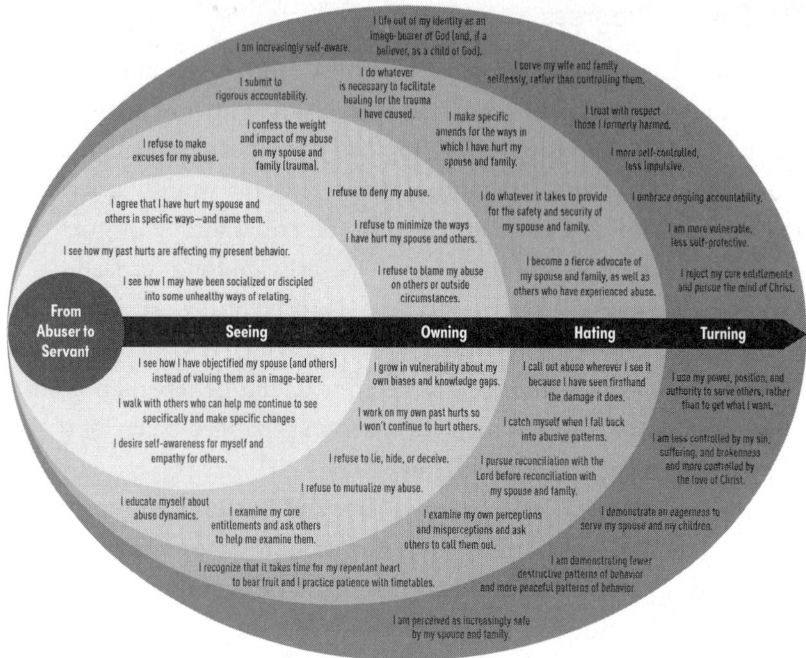

Diagram showing behavioral markers of abusive person turning from his sin.[11]

Seeing

The repentance journey begins with the abusive person **seeing** himself and his behaviors rightly. There can be no genuine repentance if the sin cannot be accurately seen and named. In this process with a couple, you have probably already heard the abused spouse's concerns about specific behaviors that she has labeled abusive or destructive. The abuser cannot repent if he cannot see and name these behaviors for himself. Does he agree that he has hurt his partner (and potentially others) in specific ways? Does his list of destructive behaviors comport with hers? Of course, it is possible for the two partners to have different perspectives on things that happened. But part of this process is to try to reconcile what the abused spouse has experienced as abusive behaviors with what the abuser believes that he did. Perhaps some of

11. This graphic is adapted from Pierre and Wilson, *When Home Hurts*, 194–95. Used by permission.

the discrepancies between her experience and his understanding can be explained by a lack of self-awareness or a lack of empathy on his part. Does he desire to grow in self-awareness and empathy to the extent that he might be better able to see and validate her experience of him? Some discrepancies might be better understood as "blind spots." Does he walk with others in close accountability relationships who can help him continue to see his sin and make specific changes?

Perhaps some of his destructive behaviors are the result of unhealthy coping with his own trauma, like abuse or abandonment in his own past. Does he accurately perceive how his past hurts might be affecting his present behavior? In his past, he may have been taught, socialized, or even discipled (unwittingly perhaps) into unhealthy ways of relating to others. Is he willing to consider this as an option and consider ways that this may have impacted his partner's experience of him? Has he learned or developed "objectifying" ways of looking at other image-bearers? Is he willing to consider ways that he may have used others to get what he wants?

Let me issue one word of caution when you are trying to help someone see his destructive behaviors: A result of educating an abusive, manipulative, or controlling person on his destructive behaviors may be that he "weaponizes" this newfound knowledge on his partner. He may label his partner with the behaviors he has been called out for—now she is also a manipulator and an unsubmissive controller. This behavior should be warned against and challenged as further abusive behavior when it occurs.

Owning

It is significant when a person's eyes are opened to behaviors that are manipulative, controlling, harmful, harsh, critical, demeaning, or destructive in other ways. But seeing is not enough. Does he **own** his sin? Or does he *minimize*, *deny*, *rationalize*, *blame* her or others, or use other similar defense mechanisms to avoid accountability for his sin? Does he *mutualize* his sin in the marriage by continuing to point out her sin? Minimizing, denying, blaming, mutualizing, justifying, rationalizing—all of these are examples of what I call "accountability avoiders." None of us like to have our sin pointed out. It is uncomfortable at least; often it is deeply shameful. Our corrupt hearts employ a number of strategies like those named above to evade having to face our brokenness. It's much easier to talk about how broken she is than to face my own depravity.

This is nothing new. Adam blamed God and Eve (Genesis 3:12). Eve blamed the serpent (Genesis 3:13). Moses blamed the people he was supposed to be leading (Deuteronomy 3:26). And these are just a few examples of blaming from the Bible. Space won't allow me to give exhaustive examples from the Scriptures of how our sinful hearts dodge accountability for our sins. But Jesus and Paul aren't about to let us off the hook. Jesus warns us to take care of our own sin before we point out the sins of others (Matthew 7:3–5). Paul reminds us that we have no excuse when we pass judgment on others because we do the very same things (Romans 2:1, 3).

While you are trying to help a destructive person own his sin, you will find yourself constantly redirecting him from pointing you to what everyone else is doing wrong: you, the church, his wife, his community group, his accountability group. One way that you can do this is ask him to speak about his sinful behavior without giving any context. In other words, you are looking for something like, "I demeaned my wife by calling her an idiot." This is a good example of owning. What you will often get instead may be something like, "I called my wife an idiot, after she once again, just like she always does, forgot to pick up the dry cleaning. And I had an important meeting the next day! I needed that suit!" He isn't owning anything in this statement. Instead, he is actually continuing to demean his wife *to you*! Just tell him, "I don't want the context. I don't care right now about your rationalization for why you did what you did. Let's just stick to naming the behavior. Period." What you (and him) will learn as you try to practice this new accountability habit is how excruciating it feels to him to just name his destructive behavior without giving you a whole story that ends up minimizing, justifying, rationalizing, blaming, denying, mutualizing, etc. "The heart is deceitful above all things, and desperately sick; who can understand it?" (Jeremiah 17:9).

If—and this is a big if—you are able to help an abusive person accurately see and own his sin, you and he have taken several big steps in the right direction. By this time, you and he are working off a list of destructive behaviors that he has seen and named that, roughly or partially, matches the ones that she has named. He has also owned at least some of these—he can name them as a sinful pattern of behaviors that have hurt his wife. He can do this without giving you a whole story about why he did what he did—that is a not-so-veiled attempt to squirm out of having to face accountability for his sin.

Hating

He and you now face a new challenge. Is he coming to **hate** these behaviors? Notice the phraseology of "coming to hate." It's important. A person can see his sin and own his sin at a specific point in time. But hating sin and turning from sin doesn't just happen at a singular point in time. It is a process. We grow in hatred for our sin as we understand the weight and impact of it on those we love and as we understand how God sees it. Is he growing in understanding of why it was so hurtful to his wife? Is he starting to recognize how it may have traumatized her? This is not hatred of self or self-loathing, which would actually just be another form of spiritual pride; it is an acknowledgment that there is a better path and a better goal than self-gratification, that the old ways of relating did damage to himself and those around him, and that he wants to relate to others in a new way that is desirable and beautiful. Commitment to continued accountability and to acting for the good, safety, and protection of others is part of this stage.

Making amends is also a key part of this stage. This specifically entails going to the people hurt by his past abusive actions and confessing and owning that behavior, as well as doing whatever can be done to make it right. The best biblical example of amends as evidence of repentance is the story of that "wee little man" Zacchaeus in

Luke 19. You know the story about Zac climbing into the sycamore tree to see Jesus and Jesus inviting himself to Zac's house. Remember what Zac did as evidence of his repentance from essentially stealing money from people while he worked as a tax collector for Rome? "Behold, Lord, the half of my goods I give to the poor. And if I have defrauded anyone of anything, I restore it fourfold" (Luke 19:8). Zac was so impacted by Jesus that he calls him Lord and announces that he intends to make things right. And not just right—that would only commit him to restore the wrong onefold. But not Zac. No. He is prepared to restore fourfold any fraud that he has committed. This is a beautiful picture of the concept of amends. This involves not only vulnerably in admitting to friends, relatives, and children the specific ways that the abuser manipulated, deceived, and exerted control for his own benefit, but also hatred of sin that often compels one to boldly go above and beyond to demonstrate awareness of how much pain and suffering his behavior has caused.

I know of a man who had demeaned his wife to all of their friends and family as a way of making himself look better than her. When he truly began to hate what he had done, he made a list and went to each person, with his wife, to tell them how amazing his wife is and that she had not done anything at all to deserve what he had said about her. Further, he asked each person to hold him accountable to the Ephesians 4:29 standard of only speaking words that would build up, fit the occasion, and give grace to those who hear. That is a picture of amends and hating one's sin. We also look for an increased level of self-awareness that enables the abuser to catch himself and name abusive behaviors, instead of others always having to point it out to him.

Last, growth in humility is shown by inviting others to point out corrupt behaviors he cannot see—and acting on those insights. Each of these actions is a way of "putting to death" or "hating" the corrupt perceptions and behaviors that the abuser had previously relied on, and as he does so, he is beginning to develop a new way of seeing himself and relating to others.

Turning

This fundamental change of perception and actions is expressed most clearly in the final stage of transformation: **turning**. To review, up to this point, he has been able to name his destructive behaviors (seeing), resulting in a list of destructive behaviors that is coming to match the hurts that his wife has experienced from him. And he has accepted accountability (owning), evidenced by refusing to minimize, deny, mutualize, or blame his abusive behaviors on someone else. He is growing in understanding the seriousness of his abusive behaviors as God and his wife do (hating), resulting in his making amends. Now comes the last task of turning, which is evidenced in changed behavior over time. Our biblical basis for turning should be obvious: Ephesians 4:17–32 and Colossians 3:1–17, the "putting off," and "putting on" texts. We look for a shift from old ways of behaving to new—from controlling others to giving them control and choices; from ignoring and disrespecting their words and needs to serving them; from being impulsive to growing in patience and self-control. We also look for a new sense of peace in the home and a growing sense of safety in the family. These insights should come from the victim or her advocate. Ultimately, our hope is that the abuser changes and begins to live out his identity as an image-bearer of God, and if a believer his identity as a child of God, by serving his wife and family selflessly rather than controlling them, by respecting those that he's formerly harmed, and by becoming an agent of the life, love, and peace of God to those around him.

This view of repentance in an abusive person is neither rigid nor precise, but hopefully it provides some guidelines to look to and goals to set when working with an abuser. It must be noted that this process takes a long time. If you sense that the abusive person is trying to jump ahead or rush the process, it's likely that they will be in that first phase of seeing for a long while. Sometimes the unspoken (or spoken) question you may sense is, "How long do I have to do this?" The implied rest of the question is ". . . before I can get you all to leave me alone and let me go back to handling my family the way I think best?" This type of impatience means that he doesn't yet see himself and his actions as they truly are—abusive, harmful, and corrupt. We may have to spend a lot of time in the first stage, and we may never get past it. But we can never permit ourselves to succumb to a sense of hurry or pressure; this is a long haul. An abusive person will be in this journey—like all of us they will never be perfect, but we are looking for clear signs of growth.

I'll be transparent: walking with abusive men in a process similar to the one that I have described here is exhausting. And, as I have already said, you cannot do it for long if it is all you do or if you do it alone. As a counselor, I love my work with adolescents (some think I am crazy for that), married couples for whom abuse is not a factor, men with struggles other than abusiveness, and families. Variety in the work keeps me sane. And doing this work in the community of co-laborers (like the friends collaborating with me on this book) also keeps me sane. But this work, while exhausting, is also a huge blessing. I'm not inviting you into it. If you're supposed to do this on some level, the Lord will invite you into it like he did me, and you won't have a choice at that point. If he does, he will have already provided other resources for you, like a local domestic abuse agency that offers a BIPP program,[12] local counselors who have some level of training and experience in abuse dynamics, and resources such as this book and others. Take advantage of all of the resources he has given, stay in the lane and within the bounds of what you are called and qualified to do, and remember that it is the God of peace who brings peace.

"Now may the God of peace himself sanctify you completely, and may your whole spirit and soul and body be kept blameless at the coming of our Lord Jesus Christ. He who calls you is faithful: he will surely do it" (1 Thessalonians 5:23–24).

---

12. Pierre and Wilson, *When Home Hurts*, appendix C includes a list of all the national and state domestic violence resources.

CHAPTER 10

....

Wisdom for Discerning Repentance in Oppressors[1]

Darby A. Strickland

God calls all of us to have hearts that are characterized by repentance. Jesus begins his preaching ministry with these words: "Repent, for the kingdom of heaven is at hand" (Matthew 4:17). His words call all of us to turn away from our sin and toward him. In addition to being charged with our own repentance, some of us are tasked with assessing the repentance of others. Pastors, elder boards, and counselors are often brought into situations where they need to make a determination as to whether or not a sinner is grieved by his or her transgressions and is committed to change. This responsibility can feel overwhelming, especially with abuse. The difficulty of the task is like navigating a minefield, and it often feels easier to pursue the restoration of a marriage than to confront the sin that destroys it.

Have you been fooled by incomplete apologies and then were shocked to find the oppressor returning to his or her sin? I have, and it is why I wrote this chapter. When we are fooled, there can be dire consequences. If an abusive husband verbally repents—but isn't sincere—what's at stake? The safety of his wife and children. If church

---

1. This chapter is adapted from Darby Strickland, "How to Discern True Repentance When Serious Sin Has Occurred" *Journal of Biblical Counseling* 34, no. 3 (2020): 30–47. Used with permission.

leaders and counselors encourage quick forgiveness and the family reunites, what can happen? The husband's abuse against his wife might escalate as a punishment for exposing his sin, which results in her now fearing speaking up.

We need God's wisdom. I have witnessed complex counseling cases where those involved long for an oppressor to be restored so much that it distorts the caregivers' judgment. We see what we hope to see instead of what is actually occurring. If pastors, elders, and counselors accept a standard of repentance different from the Lord's, the implications for both the oppressor and their victim are vast and devastating.

In this chapter, I will focus on discerning repentance in those who oppress their spouse. I will describe how to approach the assessment of repentance with a robust framework that cares for both the victim and the oppressor. We will look at why accurately assessing repentance is a way to love both the oppressor and their victim and then discuss how to determine whether a person's repentance is sincere or not. Finally, we will consider the components that should be present when robust repentance occurs.

Why Assess for Repentance?

Abusers are masters at using their words, and at the same time, those assessing repentance do not always know what they are looking for. Hence, victims of abuse are often asked to accept confessions, apologies, or excuses from an oppressor. The focus of the counseling then becomes how the victim can forgive and work to restore the relationship. But starting restoration work before there is robust repentance harms both parties. If a harmed person tries to rebuild a relationship with a person who continues in the same sin, he or she remains vulnerable to more abuse. Further, each new infraction erodes the repair attempts. Over time, this can lead to a layering of betrayal that can culminate in hopelessness. As for oppressors, if they continue in sin, they are not only in spiritual danger, but they will be tempted to look away from their own hearts and focus on their frustration over not being forgiven.

Let's look at an example. A wife reports that her husband was angry with her and kicked the dog. He insists he was in a hurry and *didn't really mean* to kick the animal—the dog was just in his way. When confronted, he says he does not understand why it's a big deal; the dog is fine. After brief counsel with their pastor, he apologizes by saying, "Sorry, my anger got the best of me. I did not know you cared so much about the dog." The pastor tells the wife, "Forgive him; it is not loving to keep a record of his wrongs. And stop bringing it up because reminding him of his mistake hurts him." What is wrong with his apology? We see that he offered excuses for this behavior, but he did not address his heart. He also dismissed the impact of his actions on the dog and his wife. His wife senses that something is still off, but she feels confused and guilty for struggling to forgive him. We do a disservice when we accept an oppressor's words without careful attunement to what those words indicate.

You might be uncomfortable with the idea of judging someone else's repentance, especially if the oppressor seems to say the right thing. I would argue that the oppressor should be pronouncing the loudest judgment upon themself like David did when he repented of his adultery in Psalm 51. When people truly are broken by their sin, it should be clear from the many ways they are grieved and seeking to change. Their voice should offer the loudest cry that they did something terribly wrong that hurt someone else. If this is not the case, their repentance is suspect and the most loving next step is to assess it further. The following are three compelling reasons for us to engage in an earnest assessment.

First, we assess to show love for the oppressor.

When we encounter abuse, we should be concerned with the heart of the one who perpetrates it. Scripture tells us that unless sin is dealt with, it will harden our hearts. Listen to this warning:

> Take care, brothers, lest there be in any of you an evil, unbelieving heart, leading you to fall away from the living God. But exhort one another every day, as long as it is called "today," that none of you may be hardened by the deceitfulness of sin. For we have come to share in Christ, if indeed we hold our original confidence firm to the end. (Hebrews 3:12–14)

Our hearts are either hardening against God or growing softer toward him. God's desire is for those who do not heed his Word to turn back to him, and he asks us to exhort one another toward that end. He calls us to confront the evil we see in believers' hearts out of concern for *them* (Galatians 6:1; James 5:19–20). Explaining this to victims helps them realize that helping their oppressor pursue true repentance is actually a way to love them.

We know that a heart that is not honest and repentant before the Lord suffers for it. Listen to the words of Psalm 32: "For when I kept silent, my bones wasted away through my groaning all day long. For day and night your hand was heavy upon me; my strength was dried up as by the heat of summer" (vv. 3–4). An unrepentant person cannot have peace with God. If we want to minister well to oppressors, we need to help them see that when they sin against another, they also sin against God, which has serious implications for their spiritual condition. We want to make sure they know how to restore their relationships with others—and also with the Lord.

Consider how the apostle Paul recounts his plea to the Corinthian church. He wants them to see their sin, so he expresses his heart for them in this way:

> So although I wrote to you, it was not for the sake of the one who did the wrong, nor for the sake of the one who suffered the wrong, but in order that your earnestness for us might be revealed to you *in the sight of God*. Therefore we are comforted. (2 Corinthians 7:12–13, emphasis added)

His focus is on the Corinthians' restoration with the Lord and how their grief-filled repentance brings him joy. Let this instruct us.

Further, by loving oppressors in this way, we limit their ability to sin against their spouses. If and when they do repent, they will be grateful to you for restraining their sin and the harm that they would have otherwise perpetrated.

Second, we assess in order to equip the victim with the information needed for wise decision-making.

Figuring out how to respond to your oppressor is challenging. Trust does not just reappear after your oppressor makes an apology. It has to be rebuilt. Think of a teenager who is caught stealing from his parents to pay for drugs. An apology is not enough to establish that the teen is now reformed and he won't steal from them again. Wise parents will lock up any jewelry or valuables in their home and monitor their child more closely. Assessing for concrete signs of repentance is one way we can help a victim navigate what steps to take next. Until there is evidence of true repentance, the relationship might have to change, or limits might have to be placed upon it.

Realize, too, that if victims of abuse postpone or forgo pursuing repentance, it will come at a high cost to them. If a friend gossips about me and I choose to overlook it, I run the risk of them continuing to speak poorly about me, which can cause significant pain and problems for sure! But if a spouse extends mercy to their abuser? Not only will they be subject to more abuse, but they will be living alongside someone who can harm them at any time. When we are advising victims on how to respond to being sinned against, or how long they should wait on repentance, we must have in mind the tension of desiring reconciliation and recognizing that the victim can be hurt further if the timing is wrong. Extending mercy postpones justice, likely resulting in more harm to the victim. If the oppressor has not repented, perhaps that means the victim needs to consider how the relationship should change to ensure their safety while waiting to see what God will do.[2]

Sometimes our role is to help victims wait well. As they wait, we weep and lament with them. Other times, our role is to encourage them to seek justice or implement consequences for what has occurred. Frequently, I have seen this overlooked in my work with abused women. A church asks a spouse to postpone moving out to see if her husband will repent of his brutality. But if she is not protected during this time, it is likely that she will continue to be abused. Whatever route our counsel takes, we need to have the cost to the sufferer in full view.

Third, we assess to protect the relationship of the oppressed with God.

Similar to the woman in the illustration I offered earlier, my counselees will often express guilt because even after hearing an "apology" from their abuser, they continue to struggle with feeling hurt. One reason for this is that oppressors often offer insincere or incomplete apologies. But victims believe that it is their responsibility to forgive and move on after any apology, even an incomplete one. When an abuse victim is told by the church that the abuser has repented and it is her job to forgive, and when she sees privately that there is no change, it drives a wedge between her and the Lord because it can seem like the Lord is on the abuser's side. Or in another instance there may be a sincere apology, but the hurt requires time to heal—she feels guilty because she cannot instantly forgive. Both of these victims are wrongly burdened with false guilt, and I have seen time and time again that they cut themselves off from the Lord and his care when they need it most. For these reasons we need to address

---

2. I am not suggesting that we should advise someone to postpone seeking criminal justice. For instance, we always report child abuse. I am referring here to the broader concept of justice. In fact, if a crime has been committed, you should encourage the victim to report criminal abuse to the police. They will need protection and a legal record of abuses when seeking a protective order or determining child custody.

what an oppressor's repentance should look like and suggest that an insufficient apology cannot repair serious damage.

Ministering in the context of abuse is an opportunity for us to show God's heart toward abuse, victims, and oppressors. It is not always wise to think charitably or believe the best about someone. Although we might think we should extend grace, Scripture asks us to be discerning and make careful assessments based on a person's words and actions (Matthew 7:15–20; John 7:24). When serious sins occur, all parties need the actual grace Jesus offers, and that grace is his invitation to repent and be forgiven. Therefore, to be loving is to provide counsel that leans into the exposed sin, cultivating both discernment and repentance—always having the relationship of both parties with the Lord as the focal point of our work toward restoration.

Now that we have established the reasons we should assess for repentance, we will learn how to identify the characteristics of true repentance. Let's begin though by identifying behaviors that might look like repentance but actually fall short of it.

What Repentance Is Not

What does incomplete or false repentance look like? How can we tell? Some manifestations are subtle and thus easy for us to miss. Others are more sinister distortions that confuse us and the victim. It's important to be attuned to these so that your assessment is accurate and if you have the opportunity, you can work to help foster budding repentance in the oppressor.

Let's begin by revisiting a Scripture passage we looked at earlier. Paul's heart was heavy for the people of Corinth because they had fallen into sin. He attempted a visit to help them along in their faith, but that seemed only to make things worse. He considered that visit a failure (2 Corinthians 2:1), so he had Titus bring them a letter in which he strongly rebuked them. Paul was unsure of how his message would be received. He longed for them to turn to Jesus, but he feared it would get an angry reception. Paul is just like many of us;

he did not enjoy the thought of a confrontation with these dearly loved people. He likely feared his rebuke might lead to their rejection of the Lord. We can hear his relief when Titus came back with good news of the Corinthians' longing, mourning, and zeal for him (2 Corinthians 7:7). Then Paul writes, "For even if I made you grieve with my letter, I do not regret it—though I did regret it, for I see that that letter grieved you, though only for a while" (v. 8). The grief of the Corinthians was short-lived, and it brought about earnest repentance, the best of all outcomes.

In his elation, Paul expounds upon the difference between godly regret and worldly sorrow. Understanding this difference is central to discerning repentance. These are Paul's words:

> Yet now I am happy, not because you were made sorry, but because your sorrow led you to repentance. For you became sorrowful as God intended and so were not harmed in any way by us. Godly sorrow brings repentance that leads to salvation and leaves no regret, but worldly sorrow brings death. See what this godly sorrow has produced in you: what earnestness, what eagerness to clear yourselves, what indignation, what alarm, what longing, what concern, what readiness to see justice done. At every point you have proved yourselves to be innocent in this matter. (vv. 9–11 NIV)

Here we learn that real repentance will feature *godly sorrow*. It will be evident as change in both the oppressor's mind and actions. Godly sorrow is directed by and toward God and produces outward and inward changes that lead to true repentance. But Paul also points out that we can be sorry for our sin without repenting from our sin. This is *worldly sorrow*, and it is directed toward ourselves. We regret our actions for the effect they have upon us and the consequences we face, but it produces no godly change. It is easy to regret being exposed as a sinner, but oppressors should also be expressing sorrow for the damage that they have done to another and the sin they have committed against the Lord.

The problem is that worldly grief is often falsely labeled as true repentance. This is not just dangerous for an oppressor whose heart remains unrepentant—it also creates particular vulnerabilities for the victim. I have identified five ways that we often mistake counterfeits for genuine repentance. Keeping these categories in mind when assessing someone's repentance will help guard against poor decisions and the damage that can result.

First, repentance is not a mere apology.

There are some acts an apology is suited for, such as stepping on someone's toe or inadvertently hurting a friend's feelings. But when we consider larger and repetitive sins, like abuse, an apology is not enough to repair the damage that the oppressor has done.[3] A repentant person will want to address the damage and commit to a new way of behaving.

Just think about how apologies are often framed: "I am sorry for doing X." This type of apology states what was wrong but often fails to include an acknowledgment of the harm done to the other person. This could be because the oppressor has not realized the damage yet or it could be because the oppressor hopes an apology is all that is needed for resolution. Jeremiah 9:8 cautions further that sometimes people will pretend to reconcile: "Their tongue is a deadly arrow; it speaks deceitfully; with his mouth each speaks peace to his neighbor, but in his heart he plans an ambush for him." People are capable of deceiving us with their lips. That is why we need to evaluate them carefully. Are the words specific and are they spoken by a person who is judging his or her own sin as serious?

---

3. Not all sins do the same amount of damage. The Westminster Standard Larger Catechism of Faith in Questions 150 and 151 outline why some sins are more grievous than others. Its teaching has greatly guided my thinking when I am caring for someone who is suffering a more grievous sin at the hand of another. I encourage you to consider the many categories and Scripture references it provides.

Second, repentance is not the fear of consequences.

When we have done wrong, we often fear the consequences more than we desire being right with the Lord. As we discussed earlier, this is called worldly sorrow. It is possible to show remorse that does not seek to turn away from sin patterns and restore relationships, but instead seeks to avoid the consequences of sin. In our pride, we regret making a fool of ourselves, but this remorse is self-centered or even self-preserving. I have heard many confessions of sin—and have even offered a few myself—where the focus is not upon the harm done to the other person, but rather trying to limit the looming consequences. These confessions are usually incomplete and fail to address the impact that the sin has on others and the Lord.

We need to be on guard against sorrow that is selfishly motivated and seeks to undo the potential consequences for the oppressor without any care for the victim. I have seen believers deceived by this type of self-centered sorrow when the stakes are high for the oppressor. Many perpetrators of violence against their wives can utter tear-filled apologies, begging a pastor or victim not to call the police so that he will not lose his job or go to jail. He weeps more for himself than for what he has done or for the person he hurt. These types of apologies are typically offered after being exposed or confronted. We do such people no favors when we believe them. They are in a perilous spiritual position, and we place a victim at risk of further harm.

In short, when you listen to oppressors offer apologies, discern if the apology is crafted in a way that is trying to limit the consequences they face or is a result of being caught—or whether they themselves felt convicted and confessed to their sin unprompted.

Third, repentance is not a promise to do better.

Promises not to repeat abusive behavior in the future can be encouraging—but they are not enough. Heart change does not happen by merely proclaiming, "I will not do *that* anymore!" If our hearts remain positioned to live for ourselves and not for the Lord, then sin patterns will continue. Time and time again, we will harm our neighbor to satisfy ourselves. Deuteronomy 23:21 reminds us of the danger of making oaths we do not fulfill: "If you make a vow to the LORD your God, you shall not delay fulfilling it, for the LORD your God will surely require it of you, and you will be guilty of sin." Upon hearing such promises, we should slow people down and use the opportunity to help them commit to the work of heart-level change.

Think again of the husband who kicked the dog. He might say he wants to do better. His wife, no doubt, longs for reassurance. However, until he develops distaste for his sin, understands why he uses violence, identifies his triggers, and articulates the damage it does to his relationships with God and his wife, he remains vulnerable to sinning that way again. Real repentance is not offered as a redo or a reset button. It acknowledges the pain of the past and engages in the hard, specific changes needed to fight sin patterns.

Often when victims hear the person who hurt them make promises to reform, they are either falsely reassured or uncomfortable about voicing concerns. It is therefore wise for us to help them consider if the promises are adequate or if other steps should be considered. In many churches, forgiveness is stressed without the needed commitment of the oppressor to demonstrate their desire *and ability* to extinguish sinful patterns for a long period of time. We need to think differently about how to guide the reconciliation process in cases of domestic abuse. As we care for victims, we should be honest about the depth of the sin involved and what it really will take to extinguish abusive sin patterns. Then we can invite victims to think about and interact honestly with the words they are hearing.

Fourth, repentance is not partial.

It must address the full problem. For example, say a husband is caught lying about how he spends money. He has repeatedly done so because he feels entitled to buy himself all the latest technology. He is not bothered that he is taking on debt or restricts his wife to a tiny allowance for her personal needs. He repents for lying and expresses remorse for being deceitful, but does not confess his rebellion as it relates to his entitlement and saddling his family with debt they cannot afford. And so, his destruction of the family's finances continues, perhaps with less deception than before. Instead of dealing with all of the sins involved, his destruction of the family's finances is allowed to continue.

Sometimes incomplete repentance might initially be because oppressors (and their counselors) do not always see the depths of their sin. As Scripture warns all of us, we do not know our hearts (Jeremiah 17:9–10). So we should gently try to help oppressors see the extent of their sin against God and others. We do this with the same love that God has for us, offering his sweet invitation of Jesus's forgiveness and his robes of righteousness. We do not seek to expose someone without offering the remedy God has already graciously provided. Still, after they are reproached, we have to ask whether an oppressor is only willing to own and talk about certain aspects of sin, or whether he or she is ready to address it in its entirety. In David's confession in Psalm 51, he offered his whole heart to the Lord. He asked God to search him and cleanse him. He knew his sins were vile, and he did not try to limit which ones he would deal with.

Fifth, repentance does not avoid taking responsibility or taking action.

It is not repentance when oppressors agree their behavior has upset someone but won't admit those behaviors were wrong or fail to take ownership of them. Some people are willing to say, "I did something that *you are labeling as wrong* only because *you are failing to understand* what I actually did." Here are some examples: "Sure, I called you a lazy worthless wife, but you needed some motivation to clean the house." Or "I was harsh with you, but you should have known I was joking." Perhaps they admit to what they did because they want to appear righteous or are worried about their image. But if they are not willing to do anything to address the situation (ask forgiveness and make appropriate amends), that is not true repentance.

We see a similar stance with the rich young ruler in Mark 10. He asked Jesus how to earn eternal life. But just as the man declares that he knew and kept all the commandments, people who fail to repent believe they are blameless. Jesus was tender with his blindness as he challenged him to reveal his true commitments: "And Jesus, looking at him, loved him, and said to him, 'You lack one thing: go, sell all that you have and give to the poor, and you will have treasure in heaven; and come, follow me.' Disheartened by the saying, he went away sorrowful, for he had great possessions" (Mark 10:21–22). The rich young ruler did not accept responsibility for his sin and was unwilling to make the changes Jesus required of him. Likewise, as we assess for repentance, we must listen for a confession that accepts blame and identifies what actions will be taken to demonstrate a change of heart.

Having considered these different types of false repentance, we see why Paul warns that "worldly grief produces death" (2 Corinthians 7:10). If oppressors never move beyond grief for the consequences they face, they will not see how they have offended God, and thus they will remain in a perilous spiritual position. They might regret the past or bemoan their present circumstances, but if they fail to deal with their spiritual condition, then they are likely to repeat their sins and continue to abuse their spouse.

Let's now turn our attention to the characteristics of true repentance.

What Does Real Repentance Look Like?

Though worldly sorrow is a spiritual dead end, godly sorrow is the pathway to repentance. It stands in great contrast to worldly sorrow, for it encapsulates both a change in thinking and a desire to act. Consider Zacchaeus, the crooked tax collector. After his encounter with Jesus, he repented and vowed to give back the money he took and to also return what he stole fourfold. And he decided to give half of his own possessions to the poor (Luke 19:8)! When I do domestic abuse training seminars with Chris Moles, I often hear him say, "When is a thief no long longer a thief? When he becomes a generous man!" True repentance goes beyond the expression of regret or streams of tears. It produces something. We can see it and observe it. When a person truly turns toward God and away from the things the Lord hates, we will not miss it.

While godly sorrow does not feel good, it produces good fruit. Scripture knows this and urges us not to regret bringing about true repentance in an oppressor (2 Corinthians 7:8–9). Yes, there is pain involved, but it is like the pain involved in pruning branches because it is temporary and necessary for growth and renewal (John 15:2–6).

What does real repentance entail? What should we be listening for? What should be able to see? Though no two people will repent in the same way, and circumstances are different, all expressions of true repentance should exhibit these eight characteristics.

First, the oppressor recognizes that the offense is against God.

Sin is more than an infraction of our human relationships. It violates our relationship with God. In Psalm 51, David states that his sin of adultery was against the Lord: "Against you, *you only*, have I sinned and done what is evil in your sight" (v. 4, emphasis added). There is no doubt that his adultery was also a sin against many people, but David drives the point home that his sin was first against the Lord. This type of confession is a critical aspect of true repentance.

Second, the oppressor agrees with Scripture's indictment of his or her sin.

So often I hear apologies that are lacking. I have offered some myself. Here is what they sound like:

- "Sorry if you found my words offensive."
- "I am sorry I hurt your feelings."
- "I am sad that you thought that I was ignoring you."

These words acknowledge the hurt, but they do not go far enough. When we have sinned and use Scripture as our measuring stick, we are more precise with the indictment of our sin, and our confessions and apologies will sound different:

- "My words were harsh and tore you down. I failed since I am called to build you up." (see 1 Corinthians 14:26)
- "I am sorry I was not gentle when you approached me. I failed to listen to you and was not open to reason." (see James 3:17)
- "You are right. I verbally attacked you when you reached out to me. I failed to love you as God calls me to do." (see Matthew 25:39–40)

God's Word should not just frame the injustice, but the confession of a penitent person should capture its concepts. Help an oppressor ask God to help them see their sin the way he does.

Third, the oppressor's confession offers specifics.

The more grievous the sin committed, the more critical it is for the oppressor to include specific infractions. Listen to Paul's specificity when he talks about his own sin. In Acts 26, he stands trial before King Agrippa. This is not an ideal time for him to be honest about his past, yet Paul recounts his days as a Pharisee and offers concrete details.

> On the authority of the chief priests I put many of the Lord's people in prison, and when they were put to death, I cast my vote against them. Many a time I went from one synagogue to another to have them punished, and I tried to force them to blaspheme. I was so obsessed with persecuting them that I even hunted them down in foreign cities. (Acts 26:10–11 NIV)

Oppressors often gloss over their failings. Imagine if Paul only said something such as, "Before I knew better, I made some mistakes," or "At that time, I did what I thought was right," or "I persecuted the Jews, but now I regret it." If he had done so, he would never have been able to rebuild trust with the disciples or been seen as a credible witness to Jesus. Specificity matters because it says to the victim, and to the Lord, that you know exactly what was wrong with what you did.

Here is an example of a confession that offers specifics: "I now recognize I often interrupt you and talk over you. That must make you feel devalued and dismissed. I do not want you to think that your thoughts don't matter to me. I have been foolish to think I always know what is best. I am going to try not to interrupt you because I believe your opinions and counsel are valuable. If I do it again, please tell me because I need and want to hear what you have to say."

Fourth, the oppressor recognizes that God's grace allows us to turn from our sins.

It is a gift to the oppressor when they know that they cannot turn from sin in their own strength. An oppressor who understands this should be able to express a humble dependence upon the Lord for his forgiveness, mercy, and power. When an oppressor moves away from self-reliance, we will witness a turning toward God and a growing interest in the Word, prayer, and other people (1 Thessalonians 1:9). At the same time, we want to guard against an oppressor who might manipulate this by saying that they are waiting on the Lord to change them, allowing them to remain passive.

Fifth, the oppressor possesses a strong desire to dismantle the old, sinful self.

A repentant person actively puts to death all that is evil, including anything that inches him or her toward it. At the same time, a repentant person will cultivate new desires to replace fallen ones. The truly repentant are committed to a process. They do not think of repentance as an event, but as a new way to live. They are persistent in the pursuit of holiness. We see the opposite with the Pharisees, who wanted position and righteousness without taking up their crosses and perpetually dying to self (Luke 9:23–24; 18:9–14). Paul, on the other hand, continually confessed his sin while regularly forsaking his desires (Acts 22:4; 1 Corinthians 15:9; Galatians 1:13; 1 Timothy 1:13). To root out sin, the oppressor seeks to abandon self-righteousness and self-deception.

Sixth, the fear of the Lord is increasing in an oppressor's heart.

An oppressor is not just growing in distaste of his or her sin but is also growing in love for and fear of the Lord (Psalm 97:10). While rejoicing in God's mercy and grace, an oppressor fears, takes comfort in, and reveres God's justice, holiness, and sovereignty. Recognizing the Lord's true place and character helps dethrone self-centeredness and draws us to a right relationship with him. This radically new worship orientation is pivotal to the process of change in the oppressor's heart.

Seventh, the oppressor wholly acknowledges the specific effects of his or her sin on all the lives it touched.

Repentant oppressors have the people they harmed on the forefront of their minds. They see how their abuse impacts not just their spouse, but their children. They do what is needed to help heal those they have wounded. They are broken over what they have done and the damage that remains. They do not expect or demand to be received back into a relationship without doing the work of restoration. Their concern shifts away from themselves and is focused on those who have been harmed by them, even if that means accepting that they have damaged the relationship beyond repair.

Eighth, the oppressor is patient while others verify his or her repentance.

The truly repentant will not express frustration with the time it takes to rebuild trust. As they wait, they demonstrate the fruits of the spirit—patience, kindness, gentleness, and self-control (Galatians

5:22–23). They will readily acknowledge that it is right for others to verify that their changes are deep and long-lasting. For instance, when Jacob repented before Esau, he did not expect to receive compassion and mercy (Genesis 32). He expected and thought it reasonable for Esau to act in a self-protective manner.

Questions to Help Assess Repentance

When someone is genuinely repentant, the eight characteristics detailed are present in increasing measure. To succinctly capture what we've covered, I've written a series of questions to help assess someone's repentance. Some questions can be converted to ask the oppressor directly. Other questions are to be used in the assessment process by the oppressor's pastor, counselor, or people familiar with the situation.

- Does the oppressor confess their abuses without blame-shifting or minimizing?
- Is the confession specific and detailed?
- Is the oppressor grieved for how he or she has sinned against God?
- Is the oppressor willing to abandon self-deception?
- When wresting with old sin patterns, does the oppressor confess before being caught?
- When caught, does the person confess immediately (or soon after) and thoroughly?
- Does the truth flow from the oppressor or does it need to be pulled out?
- Does the oppressor use scriptural categories for his or her failures?
- Has the oppressor stopped justifying their sin?
- Is the oppressor growing in fear of the Lord?
- Is the oppressor relying on grace or personal performance for deliverance from sin?

- Does the oppressor have a willingness and eagerness to make amends?
- Does the oppressor understand that it is essential to demonstrate change before a relationship can be restored?
- Is the oppressor patient with their spouse, avoiding pressure or guilt to broker forgiveness or end a separation?
- Does the oppressor confess sin even when serious consequences would result?
- Does the oppressor accept the consequences?
- Do you see the oppressor seeking help and embracing accountability, pastoral rebuke, or church discipline?
- Do you observe that the oppressor is humble and teachable and seeking to learn from God, his Word, and people?

To summarize, these criteria and questions are ways to discern where someone is on the spectrum of repentance. Is this person truly acknowledging guilt, or are their statements revealing a thin commitment to change? These questions can also be used to guide you to see where you might help an oppressor grow in godly sorrow and repentance.

Offer Godly Help with Godly Wisdom

This chapter has explored how to discern the presence of true repentance in an oppressor. This is an important part of our job as helpers, but it is not always the only job. It may be that we have the blessed opportunity to help cultivate an oppressor's repentance, especially if it's there in budding form. When you see a few good signs of change, look for ways to foster more of them while gently pursuing areas where blindness, self-reliance, or pride remains. I intend for this chapter to not merely equip you to pronounce that oppressors have failed to reach the bar, but for you to attempt to help them reach it. We must seek to do more than reveal sin to the people we minister to. We must also proclaim to them the gospel of hope and change. Remind them that "God shows his love for us in that while we were *still sinners*, Christ died for us" (Romans 5:8). We all begin at the same place—at the foot of the cross. It is there that God forgives and embraces us.

But you must also temper mercy with wisdom. There might come a time where you realize an oppressor's commitment to sin, deception, and self-protection is more significant than their desire to change and love the Lord. Recognize that you cannot help those whose hearts are hardened and do not see their need of Jesus. Pray for wisdom for how long you should keep attempting to bring sight to such blindness and realize that without repentance, reconciliation may not be possible. Though God highly values renewed marriages, intact families, and united churches, he also calls us to protect the vulnerable. May God give us great wisdom so we can offer well-informed counsel to both the victim and the oppressor.

CHAPTER 11

Children and Domestic Abuse

Darby A. Strickland

One of my son's obsessions is Tesla vehicles. He is fascinated by videos where a Tesla maneuvers to avoid a potentially horrific crash. After watching videos with him, I can see why. I have been in a few car accidents myself. There is this moment when the danger is coming at you. You have to deal with the most significant threat first. You make choices based on what you see. Unlike us, a Tesla is smart enough to see and sense everything. It perceives all the risks. In an instant, it executes a calculated navigation to avoid an accident. It does not swerve to avoid one thing, only to hit another.

Please think of this chapter as me programming your minds and hearts to see and address risks to children when we encounter domestic abuse. God creates children to be like him. They, too, bear his image. They are his precious children, and we need to steward them well (Genesis 1:27; Psalm 100:3). When children grow up in a home where domestic abuse occurs, they are shaped and impacted by the evil around them. Sadly, they are also at significant risk of being direct victims of abuse. As Christians, we are told to carry each other's burdens (Galatians 6:2). This chapter will help you know how to start doing this for children who have endured domestic abuse.

The gospel is powerful enough to address childhood trauma. Healing can happen. But children are very vulnerable, and as this book demonstrates, there is already much to attend to in domestic abuse cases. So we will need to be purposeful in addressing their needs. As Christians, we know the most critical impact on people is how the gospel shapes them. So while you are learning about how domestic abuse affects children, please do so with the hope that the love and care of Jesus and the Christian community can significantly mediate these impacts.

Before we look at specific impacts, we must understand that children are prone to replicate what they see. I remember the first time my children imitated me when they were frustrated. It was eye-opening and convicting! My children had learned to respond to their world by watching me.

Earlier in this book, you have learned how coercive control works and how a victim responds to abuse. By perusing the following sampling of what children witness in their homes, you will quickly see how witnessing abuse shapes a child's view of themselves and the world around them:

- Lying keeps you safe.
- Violence solves problems.
- Shaming another person is an effective means to get your way.
- Value is based on gender.
- Verbal abuse and violence are good ways to express frustration and anger.
- Manipulating others is the norm.
- People cannot be trusted.
- We should not expose evil, but endure it.
- Numbing out is how we deal with stress and conflict.
- Non-consensual behavior is acceptable.
- Sex is used to negotiate safety and solve problems.
- We don't own our sin and repent, but instead make excuses and blame shift.[1]

The above list represents the potential worldview that children learn in their homes. On top of how witnessing abuse can shape their

1. List modified from Darby Strickland, *Is It Abuse?: A Biblical Guide to Identifying Domestic Abuse and Helping Victims* (Phillipsburg, NJ: P&R, 2020), 261.

thinking, they are also impacted emotionally, relationally, and physically by being exposed to abuse. For many, the level of exposure can be traumatizing.[2] Here is a list of impacts that may be short-term or long-term:

Emotional impacts: Children might wrestle with fear, anger, depression, shame, and paralyzing guilt. Children often believe they are responsible for the abuse. Often, they witness arguments about their discipline, grades, and financial needs, adding to their belief that the abuse is their fault.

Relational impacts: Children might struggle to build trust, find themselves isolated, have poor social skills, and possess anger toward the oppressed, oppressor, and their siblings. Their family often keeps secrets and lies to cover up the abuse, so they fear disclosing it and resist getting help.

Children might make unhealthy allegiances. They can side with the abuser to prevent being abused by them or because they have adopted the abuser's attitudes. Sometimes they even become complicit in the mistreatment. Conversely, they might become protective of the abused parent. This can lead the child to take on an adult role in the home. They might be emotionally enmeshed with the victim parent or step into the middle of an altercation. The lessons they learn at home make them susceptible to continuing the cycle of abuse as adults. Children who witness domestic violence are more likely to be affected by violence as adults—either as victims or perpetrators.[3]

---

2. Exposure to childhood domestic abuse can result in complex trauma. But assessing the source of the trauma is compounded when the child has also experienced direct physical or sexual abuse.

3. Etienne G. Krug et al., eds., *World Report on Violence and Health* (Geneva: World Health Organization, 2002), https://www.who.int/publications-detail-redirect/9241545615; Marianne James, "Domestic Violence as a Form of Child Abuse: Identification and Prevention," *Issues in Child Abuse Prevention* (June 1994), https://aifs.gov.au/resources/policy-and-practice-papers/domestic-violence-form-child-abuse-identification-and; Centers for Disease Control and Prevention, *Reproductive, Maternal and Child Health in Eastern Europe and Eurasia: A Comparative Report*, April 2003, https://dhsprogram.com/pubs/pdf/OD28/00FrontMatter.pdf; David Indermaur, "Young Australians and Domestic Violence," *Trends and Issues in Crime and Criminal Justice* 195 (2001), https://www.aic.gov.au/publications/tandi/tandi195.

Physical impacts: Children might suffer from headaches, bed-wetting, trouble eating, weight loss/gain, physical injuries (from being caught in the crossfire), and trouble sleeping.

Developmental impacts: Children might have problems concentrating, experience developmental delays, behave in disruptive or manipulative ways, or have difficulty at school.

Reactive impacts: Children often respond to traumatic experiences by being truant from school, running away, self-harming, becoming sexually active, and using drugs and alcohol. They are at higher risk for teen pregnancy and PTSD.

Spiritual impacts: Christians who grow up in homes where oppressors appear pious in public and oppress their spouses in private live daily with the poison of hypocrisy. If the church is unaware of what is happening at home and embraces the oppressor or is aware but mishandles care, further danger is done to a child's faith development. Children see a false gospel that significantly damages the testimony of Christ and interferes with their ability to trust and relate to God.

When you are counseling a child who has witnessed or experienced domestic abuse, work to discover how the abuse has affected that particular child. Though the impacts are vast, there is no one single way that all children respond to living in an abusive environment, and the intensity of the effect varies significantly from child to child. Even children living in the same home can have different responses.

Several factors can influence the severity of the impacts (age, socioeconomic status, birth order, frequency and form of abuse, duration of exposure, existence of supportive relationships, and cultural beliefs). Generally, preschool-aged children tend to have physical and anxiety-based symptoms. School-age children tend to show stress along behavioral and emotional dimensions, and teenagers tend to be at risk of seeking relief destructively (drugs, sexual activity, running away).

Due to the enormous stress and confusion that victims of abuse live with, the belief that a two-parent home is always best for a child, and the church's condemnation of divorce, many victims often fail to see the impact of domestic abuse on their children until the damage is significant. Many victims believe that their children are unaware of the abuse they endure. But when asked, 90 percent of children report being very aware of the abuse, even if it does not happen in their presence.[4] A good counselor must guide a parent to help them see and address the damage that has been done to their children.

Childhood Domestic Abuse and Child Abuse

Many children who live in homes where domestic abuse takes place are at greater risk of being physically or sexually abused by someone inside or outside their home. Children who have suffered from domestic abuse will most likely experience one or more of the following adverse childhood experiences in their childhood home: physical abuse, sexual abuse, physical neglect, emotional neglect, divorced parents, parental alcohol and drug abuse, having a mentally ill parent or an incarcerated parent.[5] This list showcases the risks of enduring domestic abuse as a child. Sixty-five percent of adults that abuse their partner also physically or sexually abuse their children.[6] It is child abuse if a parent is holding a child while that parent is attacked, if a child gets hit by objects that are thrown (even if they were not the intended target), or if they witness a parent being sexually assaulted. Further, a child's needs for clothes, food, and medical care are sometimes neglected due to financial abuse and coercive control. These are all reportable offenses.

4. "National Statistics Domestic Violence Fact Sheet," NCADV: National Coalition Against Domestic Violence, accessed July 26, 2022, https://ncadv.org/STATISTICS.

5. "Effects of domestic violence on children," Office on Women's Health, retrieved January 25, 2023, https://www.womenshealth.gov/relationships-and-safety/domestic-violence/effects-domestic-violence-children.

6. "Domestic Violence and Child Abuse," Children's Hospital of Philadelphia Center for Violence Prevention (September 21, 2022), https://violence.chop.edu/domestic-violence-and-child-abuse#:~:text=Domestic%20Violence%20and%20Child%20Abuse%20Statistics,United%20States%20occur%20at%20home.

Reporting Child Abuse

Reporting child abuse is not just mandated. It is essential (Romans 13:1–6).[7] But doing so increases the level of danger to the victim and child. To plan for their protection, you must consider the increased risk to the child and abused parent. Here are a few things you will need to know:

- Is there violence in the home, and has it escalated?
- Has the child been injured?
- Have any threats been made to harm or kill the child? Or mother?
- Has the abuser used or threatened to use weapons?
- Has the abuser threatened suicide?

These factors place the child and victim in more danger. Consulting with an advocate or domestic violence shelter is wise.[8] When you report child abuse, it will be investigated, making the situation more volatile, so you should involve experts to help you determine and execute a safety plan.

Before you make a report:

1. Discuss the risks you see with the oppressed parent.
2. Ask what they fear occurring when the report is made.
3. Inform the parent that you will report the abuse so they can be prepared and seek safety. (Depending on the level of danger the parent and children are in, they might need to leave home.)

When making a report, try to involve the oppressed parent in making the call unless you believe that filing the report together will put them at increased risk. It is wise to inform the child welfare agency about the abuse and the fears that you and the abused have.

---

7. For further guidance in reporting child abuse, you can call your county's Child Advocacy Center (www.nationalcac.org), visit www.churchcares.com, or call Childhelp National Child Abuse Hotline: 800-422-4453. The 24/7 hotline that offers confidential counseling, information, and referrals for families and advocates about all forms of child abuse.

8. The National Domestic Hotline (1-800-799-SAFE [7233]) or your local shelter can help make a safety plan.

Make sure that you name the abusive parent as the person responsible for the child abuse. The abused parent may be charged with neglect or "failure to protect" their children. Having them report the abuse with you can help manage this. Be careful not to make the report in front of the child, regardless of how young the child is, and limit the number of people who know. We do not want to alert the abuser.

After a report is made, you need to check with the abused to see how it impacted the family and if new safety concerns are arising. Always report any new allegations of abuse. The most dangerous time for a mother and her children is when she is fleeing the abuse,[9] so even if a safety plan has been enacted, changes might need to be made.

Ministry Priorities for Children

Jesus showed his value and care for children when he invited the little children to come to him even over his disciple's objections (Mark 10:13–16). He demonstrated that we need to tend to children, bless them, and willingly allow interruption by them and their needs. Jesus's heart impresses upon us that we should seek to have children directly in our view. They are image-bearers of God. Accordingly, they deserve dignity and protection. Here are some ways to help children who have witnessed domestic abuse.

Reassure them that God is present

Sometimes revelations of domestic abuse come directly from children. Other times, we seek to provide children with supportive care after we have learned about abuse in their homes. Regardless of how it comes up, children need to know that they are safe and that getting

---

9. Laurie Udesky, "U.S. Divorce Child Murder Data," Center for Judicial Excellence, May 4, 2023, https://centerforjudicialexcellence.org/cje-projects-initiatives/child-murder-data/#:~:text=Experts%20in%20domestic%20violence%20have%20long%20known%20that,front%20lines%20of%20a%20dangerous%20and%20volatile%20epidemic. See also, "Myths & Facts about Domestic Violence," Domestic Violence Intervention Program, accessed August 31, 2019, http://www.dvipiowa.org/myths-facts-about-domestic-violence/. Women are 70 times more likely to be killed in the weeks after leaving their abusive partner than at any other time during the relationship.

support for their family is good. But be careful not to promise them good outcomes, for we do not know if their abusive parent will repent and their family will be made whole. But you can reassure them that God is an ever-present help in times of trouble (Psalm 46:1).

Children need permission to reveal secrets and should have a broad understanding of what you will do with the information they disclose. For instance, they should know that you want to protect them, but you cannot keep secrets when their safety is an issue. How you handle the information they share will require lots of wisdom, so be clear about what they can expect from you and what will happen next.

Move at their pace

Children are victims too. So use the same general guidelines that apply to victims. Move at their pace and give them room to speak of both the good and bad about each parent. Do not immediately try to reinterpret what they are sharing. Be very focused on the questions that they initiate. For example, when the youth pastor first approached Sara, she was reluctant to talk about what was happening. Eventually, she started to share her confusion and fears but was still quick to defend her father. It was important that the youth pastor first listened to her concerns and her questions, and then helped her label each parent's behaviors in biblical categories. It took several long conversations before she could see her pastor's concern and care for both her parents. Once she understood this, Sara was willing to talk about how her father's sin patterns impacted her.

Ask specific questions

When interviewing a child about the abuse, utilize direct and specific questions. Here are some questions you can ask children to help them talk about what is happening at home:

1. What happens when your parents disagree?
2. What does your dad or mom do when they are angry?
3. Does anyone hit, shove, or push? Does anyone yell? Does anyone throw or break things?

4. Has anyone gotten hurt or injured?
5. Has anyone threatened to hurt someone? What did the person say?
6. What makes you feel scared or angry?
7. What do you do when they are arguing?
8. Have you tried to stop a fight? What happened?
9. Do you worry about Mom or Dad?
10. What do you do to cope with the stress?

Younger children might be more responsive to role-play or drawing.

1. Can you draw a picture of your family?
2. Can you use figures to show me what you saw?
3. Can you draw out the dreams you have for your family?
4. If you were a superhero, what would you do?

After an abuse disclosure, you will want to reassure the child that they are brave and God-honoring for speaking the truth (Ephesians 5:11). Initially, you should not use the word *abuse* with children. Stick with the verbs and adjectives that they used to describe their parents' behaviors. If safety issues or child abuse are revealed, you need to address those immediately.

Safety Planning with Children

After learning more about what is happening at home, you might need to form a safety plan. It is ideal to do it with the abused parent.[10] Whether a safety plan is formed or not, you should directly teach the child safety skills.

Coach the child on how to call 911 in an emergency. Depending on the age of the child and their ability to be discreet or keep secrets, you might want to limit talking about the abuse specifically. Avoid saying things like "Call 911 when Daddy hurts Mommy." Instead say,

---

10. Darby Strickland, *Is It Abuse?: A Biblical Guide to Identifying Domestic Abuse and Helping Victims* (Phillipsburg, NJ: P&R, 2020), 310–17. Here she gives an example of a safety plan with children in view.

"This is how to call 911 if there is an emergency like when someone gets hurt or you worry someone might get hurt." Instruct them not to step into a fight. Help them to identify a safe place to go (inside the home or with a trusted neighbor) when they are afraid. Revisit with them when, how, and who to contact in an emergency. Remember that after separation, the risk for lethal violence to mother and child dramatically increases, as does the abuser's ability to perpetrate child abuse.

Once the child's physical safety has been addressed, you can move toward caring for the child holistically.

Initial Counseling Goals for Children

There are two initial priorities for your work with children or teens who have lived or are living in homes with domestic abuse. One is to determine whether, like most children, they blame themselves for the abuse. Listen carefully to their reasoning, then help them understand that the behaviors they are witnessing are not their fault. Show them in Scripture where God says people are responsible for their own sin (Matthew 7:17; James 1:14–15). Second, spend time discovering how the distress impacts them and what coping strategies they employ. You will want to tenderly address any coping mechanisms detrimental to their well-being or Christian walk (drinking, sexual promiscuity, screen addictions, etc.).

Over time, as you build trust and a child is talking more about the abuse and its impacts, you can move toward providing them with a biblical interpretation of their world, their suffering, and eventually the abusive dynamics they endured. I can only mention this goal in passing in the chapter, but it is crucial. The child will likely need to revisit these conversations as they move through different developmental stages. Remember, they live (or have lived) in a home where the victim is blamed for everything, where there is rampant confusion, and where reality is distorted. You will also need to help them sort out their complex feelings for both parents. Michael Emlet's book, *Saints,*

Sufferers, and Sinners: Loving Others as God Loves Us (New Growth Press, 2021), will be beneficial in providing biblical frames for the messy, broken people they love.

Sometimes the abuser will intentionally impress upon their children unjustified negative opinions and interpretations of the oppressed parent. The desired result is to damage the child's relationship with the targeted parent. This is another way that abusers harm their spouses—by turning the child against them. If these behaviors are present, they will most likely increase during a separation or after a divorce. Be alert to items on the following list:

1. A child expressing relentless criticism or hatred of the targeted parent
2. A child using similar language to the alienating parent
3. A child rejecting time with (or visitation) of the targeted parent
4. A child who is emotionally enmeshed with the oppressive parent and defensive of them
5. A child with unfair or irrational judgment about the targeted parent
6. A child who can see no good in the targeted parent
7. A child who has no empathy for the targeted parent

Parental alienation is a form of emotional child abuse. The potential impact of this abuse on a child's life is a diminished ability to establish and maintain future relationships, as well as guilt, anxiety, and depression related to losing a relationship with a parent they loved. The impacts described at the beginning of this chapter also apply to this type of situation. Parental alienation is challenging to address and is best done with a counselor with training in this area. Several secular resources are available to help with this devastation.[11]

---

11. Amy J. L. Baker and Paul R. Fine, *Surviving Parental Alienation: A Journey of Hope and Healing* (Lanham, MD: Rowman & Littlefield, 2017); Amy J. L. Baker, J. Michael Bone, and Brian Ludmer, *The High-Conflict Custody Battle: Protect Yourself and Your Kids from a Toxic Divorce, False Accusations, and Parental Alienation* (Oakland, CA: New Harbinger, 2014); Amy J. L. Baker and Paul R. Fine, *Co-parenting with a Toxic Ex: What to Do When Your Ex-Spouse Tries to Turn the Kids Against You* (Oakland, CA: New Harbinger, 2014).

When parents cannot agree on a custody schedule or child support the court system often needs to be involved in settling these disputes, yet they often fail to identify or produce helpful interventions when parental alienation occurs. Oppressors are quite skilled at using the court system to their advantage.

Building a Child's Resilience

Interventions for children of domestic violence is a new field of study, but early research points to three critical factors as producing better outcomes for children of domestic violence.

Protection

Children who are protected from domestic abuse do better. It is often an older sibling who shields their younger siblings. But victims also take steps to protect their children. Sometimes this looks like sending children to grandparents for a break or scheduling activities so they are not in the home as much.

Protection also comes from fleeing abuse. But many victims fear the harm done to their children will increase because they will not be there to protect them during visitation. So they choose to stay in the abusive marriage. Removing the child completely from the abusive environment is ideal but not always easily executed, which is one reason many victims will endure abuse. Those who are not ready to leave will also shield their children by enduring abuse to keep their spouse from taking his anger out on the children. While this is noble, it is not a good long-term strategy. For example, many women endure sexual abuse so that their spouses do not punish their children when sexual entitlements are unmet. However, over time, being sexually abused greatly impacts the mother's ability to function well and, eventually, her trauma impacts her ability to parent her children.

Support

Supportive relationships that center around the child's interests and provide them with a reprieve from the abuse are invaluable. But children often want to talk about the abuse. So also identify wise Christians who can come alongside them and help them process and think biblically about abuse. Utilize the church to help set up a care team for the children. If the abuser is a male, it is essential that the children have godly men model what it looks like to be a Christian man. Outside support will give the child someone who offers sound guidance and instills Christian values amid the relational chaos. Remember, abusive people often use children to accomplish their punishments. They frequently seek to fracture the parent–child relationship. Adding outside support can help a child process these dynamics so that their relationship with their abused parent can be restored.

Agency

Abuse takes away choices, leaving victims feeling powerless. Part of healing is helping victims restore their God-given dominion or personal agency. When we experience suffering, we have choices about how we respond. Children are often captive victims with little power to effect change, but they too are called to lives that glorify the Lord and honor him. God wants them to be active in their worlds in the ways that they can be (Psalm 5:11; Proverbs 4:23). Here are some ways you might help them be engaged in resisting abuse and its impacts:

- Help them manage their complex emotions and bodily responses.
- Connect them to creative outlets for play and expression.
- Ask them to choose what support they want.
- Collaborate with them about who they talk about the abuse with and how they will talk about it.
- Involve them in safety planning.
- Teach them how to cry out to the Lord in their distress.

Lead them gently in other biblical ways to respond to deep suffering, giving them the hope that God will redeem their story.[12]

Counseling Goal for Parents

In addition to ministering to children directly, you should look for ways to help the child's parents to fulfill their God-given role in shepherding their children (Deuteronomy 6:7).

Goals for the oppressed

As you work with the oppressed, consider these counseling goals:

1. Victims need to grow in awareness of how the abuse affects their children (Jeremiah 48:4). Most victims I have worked with cannot make these connections without guided help. Ask these questions:
    - Do you think your children are aware of the abuse?
    - What do your children do when they witness abuse?
    - How do your children feel about what is happening?
    - What do you fear?
2. Check in on how discipline is happening in the home (Proverbs 22:6). In addition to the multitude of typical parenting errors we all make, I have witnessed oppressed parents make a number of reactive errors in their parenting due to the abuse they are experiencing or have experienced. Some parents react with harsh and strict discipline in hopes of meeting oppressive parents' expectations and thereby avoiding their punishments. Harsh parenting can also take place because victims wrongly misplace their anger. Others react with passive, permissive parenting because they have no energy left or they feel powerless. Sometimes a role reversal occurs since the abused parent is

12. Additional resources on counseling children who have experienced domestic abuse include Carol Santana McCleary, *The Day My Daddy Lost His Temper: Empowering Kids That Have Witnessed Domestic Violence* (Scotts Valley, CA: CreateSpace Independent Publishing, 2014); Althea T. Simpson, *Hurt to Healing: Child Witnesses of Domestic Violence and Their Invisible Injuries* (Altona, Canada: Friesen Press, 2022).

so depressed that the child takes on the parenting role. In these cases, they often make the child their confidant. Many times, even their best parenting is ineffective because their children have been taught to disrespect and mock the abused parent or they are unable to be consistent with expectations.

3. Help victims think about the longer-term impacts of the abuse on their children (Psalm 11; Proverbs 3). Many victims have been told it is best for their children if they remain married. However, this is not usually the case. I have worked with many women who choose to stay for the sake of their children, only to see their children walk away from their faith as adults and struggle with the numerous impacts outlined earlier. Intact abusive homes remain abusive. So keeping the family together should not be the metric used to determine what is best for the children. Instead, you must unpack what is actually in their child's best interest. Many factors will need to be considered.
4. Coach a victim on how to talk to the child about the abuse occurring in the home (Ephesians 4:15). Not knowing what should be said is a significant barrier to victims shepherding their children through the abuse. You can model for them how to speak about sinful behaviors, while keeping in mind that their abusive spouse is an image-bearer. You will want them to be honest but God-honoring.
5. Encourage needed reporting (Ephesians 5:11–12). Abused parents often fear involving legal authorities for two reasons: First, they worry that reporting will likely lead to increased abuse. They are usually right about this so address that with safety planning. Second, they fear they will lose custody because their oppressor often threatens to call child protective services or says they will take their children away. This threat rings true for them. Since everyone else seems to believe their oppressor and the lies he tells, the victim doubts she will be believed. Victims often point to a moment when they lost it with their children and fear their worst moment being exposed. Address

their fears and coach them to involve the police and child welfare agencies when appropriate. This not only protects their children from abuse, but also creates a needed trail of legal documentation verifying the presence of abuse. If they wait until a custody dispute to bring these issues forward, the courts will most likely see their testimony as retaliatory and dismiss them.

6. Provide hope (Psalm 9:9). Remind them that intervention improves outcomes. They have been appointed as undershepherds and can help their child through trauma.[13] But most importantly, God is at work. He desires justice for the oppressed and cares about the downtrodden and their children.[14] Then he continues to care through the healing process.[15]

Goals for the oppressor

You should consider these counseling goals if the oppressor is engaged in the change process. We want to encourage complete repentance of the abuse and look forward to restoration. At the same time, we should be encouraged to foster even minor improvements. Any improvement an oppressor makes will mean less abuse and possibly an improved relationship with both parents. So seek to counsel anywhere there is openness.

If the abuser is resistant or hostile to change, a determination will need to be made about which goals can be engaged with safely and without causing more harm to the child or oppressed parent. Considering what you can address, take special care that you are

---

13. Darby Strickland, *Something Scary Happened: Helping Children Through Trauma* [children's book] (Greensboro, NC: New Growth Press, 2023); and Darby Strickland, *When Children Experience Trauma: What to Do When Something Scary Happens* [minibook] (Greensboro, NC: New Growth Press, 2023). These books can help parents walk with their traumatized child.

14. Strickland, *Is It Abuse?*, 268–81. My book devotes time to helping mothers identify the impact of domestic abuse on their children and provides concrete ways for a mother to come alongside her children by offering protection, support, and agency.

15. Lundy Bancroft, *When Dad Hurts Mom: Helping Your Children Heal the Wounds of Witnessing Abuse* (New York: Berkley, 2005). This secular resource provides wisdom for parents who have already addressed the abuse.

not providing information that empowers and gives oppressors more ammunition.

Consider these counseling goals for an oppressor:

1. Teach healthy parenting skills. Before addressing the heart issues, you can begin by offering parenting skills and strategies. Teach ways they can address discipline issues by working to eradicate anger and their reactivity (Ephesians 4:26, 31).
2. Discourage physical discipline. When someone is coercively controlling, they should not utilize any form of physical discipline. Help oppressors brainstorm other effective and reasonable consequences (Psalm 37:8; Ephesians 6:4; 2 Timothy 2:22; James 1:20).
3. Confess coercive tactics used in parenting. Help oppressors identify ways that they manipulate their children. Do they use money, sulking, anger, threats, or cruelty to control their children? Help them be specific in their confessions by providing concrete examples.
4. Address their demand for respect. Disrespect is a hot button for oppressors and leads to explosive interactions. Assist them in understanding that God calls them to serve their children, not subject them to their entitlements (Ephesians 6:4). Even Jesus woos us with his love and care. He does not demand respect from us but gently calls us to a life of obedience.
5. Instill empathy. Oppressors tend to be self-absorbed so they will need help learning to see the world from their child's vantage point. Aid them in making the connection that their behavior impacts their children's responses to them and their world. Once they can see their child's perspective, teach them how to lead their child with compassion (Galatians 5:22–23; 6:10).
6. Encourage involvement. Many oppressors expect the benefit of a relationship with their children without putting in the work. As an oppressor is learning to love well, prompt them

to engage in the challenges and sacrifices of parenting (Luke 9:23–24).

7. Address attitudes about the oppressed. They must address their heart attitude if they have disparaged or alienated their co-parent to their children. Teach them how to repent and value their co-parent (Colossians 3:12–13).[16]

Counseling Goals for Adults Who Suffered Childhood Domestic Violence

One population that often gets overlooked is the adult survivors. They are trying to move through life with the abusive worldview they grew up with alongside the impacts of childhood trauma, and it often proves too difficult. I have counseled many people who fall into this category. Here are some things I have heard them say:

- "I do not feel like I am worth anything."
- "I feel like everything bad is my fault."
- "I just cry so easily."
- "I lash out verbally—keeping the anger in is too dangerous."
- "I do not know who I am."
- "If I can serve others, I feel OK. Otherwise, I feel useless."
- "When I am supposed to be happy, I can't be."
- "My childhood was stolen."
- "It is hard for me to talk about difficult things."
- "I lie because I don't want to start a fight."
- "I feel like I am emotionally always on edge."

One theme I have found is that victims tend to blame and be disgusted with themselves as adults. This pattern developed because of what they witnessed and because it became habitual for them to conceal their experiences. One of my counselees put it this way: "I feel

---

16. Lundy Bancroft and Jay Silverman, *The Batterer as Parent: Addressing the Impact of Domestic Violence on Family Dynamics* (Newbury Park, CA: Sage, 2002). This secular resource instructs helpers on addressing oppressors' complex impact on their children.

like I had to swallow myself up so that no one knew what was happening in my home. And now I still feel responsible for my siblings and their continued suffering because I did not expose it or fight it." This creates a great deal of internal conflict for something that they are powerless over.

As you counsel this group, consider the following goals:

1. When you have learned that you must meet your parent's expectations or expect punishment, you devote your energy to pleasing that parent. Sometimes that operational philosophy infects other relationships, and you do not learn how to relate to people. You only grow in fear of disappointing them. This mindset will lead to people-pleasing. As an adult, it might play out as not sharing your thoughts and feelings, becoming an overachiever, being fearful of disagreeing and saying no to requests from others, and feeling responsible for another's happiness. God wants us to love people and fear him (Philippians 2:12–18). It will take time to learn how to dismantle this way of thinking. But it is vital to learn how to relate to people.
2. Help them understand what they are and are not responsible for. Do not shortcut this goal. Listen for particular things that they question. Continually remind them that the abuse was not their fault.
3. Encourage them to sort out who is trustworthy. Explain what makes someone faithful and worthy of sharing the vulnerable parts of your life. Help them see when and how this should be done. Many victims overshare too soon, only to find others taking advantage of the intimate details shared. Or they close up and fear being loved. Help them grow in discerning a person's character. You will need to teach them it is good to be discerning and help them learn how to make wise evaluations of others.
4. Christians often talk about forgiveness but fail to identify when certain behaviors should change how we relate to the

people who sin against us. Teach them which sins should not be tolerated in intimate relationships. Especially in dating and engagement, we should advise that some behaviors and sin patterns are deal-breakers. Since fake and destructive love will feel more familiar, take time to explain what a healthy relationship and a genuinely repentant repair look like.

5. Adult children of domestic abuse may turn to self-harm or even addictions to address the past trauma. Do a careful inventory of how they have learned to cope and how they are currently choosing to cope with their past.
6. No doubt they will need help navigating family relationships and understanding how the dynamics of abuse played out in their home. Lead them to see how pervasive the impact was on each family member. Help them think through how to restore relationships so that they are God-honoring.
   - How can they wisely relate to each family member?
   - Who do they still need protection from?
   - As children, did they take on the role of a confidant, protector, or parent? Are they executing these roles currently?
   - Do they still carry the abuser's distortions and lies about other family members?
   - How can they let God help them find peace in the chaotic family system?
7. Shame most likely affects how they think about themselves. Remind them that their identity is secure in Christ. They need to know they are worthy, loved, and holy because of what Christ has done on their behalf. He eagerly welcomes them into his perfect and loving family.[17]

17. Anne Dryburgh, *The Emotionally Abusive Parent: Its Effects and How to Overcome Them in Christ* (Sedona, AZ: Illumine Press, 2022). This resource might be helpful in counseling adult survivors of childhood domestic abuse.

Hope for the Challenges Ahead

As we have considered how domestic abuse impacts children, we saw how God calls us to care for the littlest victims. However, your ability to provide care largely depends on the family's willingness to engage with you. At times, your burden and concern for the affected children might be greater than for their parents, and you will not be able to help in ways that you wish you could. In other moments you will be gifted with the opportunity to guide parents and children through times of protection and healing. Whatever season you find yourself in, it is important to bathe your efforts in prayer.

Do not underestimate what God will do for his children. Some days these situations will look hopeless and feel overwhelming, but nothing is too big for our God. God invites us to hope in what he will do for those he loves (Psalms 25:3; 33:20–22; 62:5–6). We should have confidence and draw strength from the fact that he is at work protecting the most vulnerable, healing the wounded, and comforting the brokenhearted. We are blessed to love and serve the vulnerable alongside him.

CHAPTER 12

....

Advocacy: God's Heart for the Helpless

Joy Forrest

Have you ever felt completely helpless? I know I have, and without the help of others, I am not sure I would have survived. When I escaped my abusive marriage in 1995, I was completely overwhelmed and powerless. For decades I had tried, and often managed, to hold everything together. But suddenly things were far beyond my control. Yet God was merciful, and during that horribly trying time, I learned that he is indeed a *very present help* in trouble (Psalm 46:1). Not only did he send people to help me with practical things like safe housing, but he began to show me his true nature through Scripture. As I was able to untwist the many lies that I had come to believe about him and myself, I was finally able to experience the peace that passes human comprehension amid great distress. My advocate in heaven made a way when there seemed to be no way. It was truly as if he "lifted me out of the miry clay and set my feet upon a rock" (Psalm 40:2 NKJV). Perhaps you can relate.

Scripture tells us that we are all helpless in a spiritual sense. "For while we were still weak, at the right time Christ died for the ungodly" (Romans 5:6). John 14:16 tells us that the Holy Spirit is our advocate, and Hebrews 7:25 tells us that Jesus "lives to make intercession" on our behalf (see also Romans 8:26–27, 34). God knows we need help, and it's important to him that we get it. Not only does he advocate on our behalf, but he commands his followers to do the same: "Defend the poor and fatherless; do justice to the afflicted and needy. Deliver the poor and needy; free them from the hand of the wicked" (Psalm 82:3–4 NKJV). These Scriptures and many more tell me that the concept of advocacy originated with God. I believe it is a mission that reflects his very heart.

Why Advocacy?

In recent years, our culture's view of advocacy has taken a different tone. The very thought of it can conjure images of extreme and angry voices that go far beyond helping the downtrodden. Instead, they attack and shame anyone who fails to completely embrace their cause. Activism of that nature does not reflect God's heart. Our helper seeks to build up, rather than tear people down—and good advocates do just that.

In a nutshell, the role of a domestic abuse advocate is to help those who have endured oppression in their homes to attain the best possible outcome in the face of devastating, and often unbearable, circumstances. The barriers these individuals face seem never-ending because domestic abuse is often counterintuitive and unclear to those they turn to for help. Helpers can be easily fooled because perpetrators of abuse can seem charming, convincing, and stable, while their victims suffer from all the symptoms of complex post-traumatic stress disorder (C-PTSD). Victims may seem overly emotional, highly defensive, and easily triggered. Many times they present as confused, overwhelmed, and unable to clearly explain what is happening at home. They may even take the blame for much of what is happening in their homes, and their partners are quick to reinforce that narrative by claiming to be the actual victims.

It's so easy to see the harsh treatment of a wife as simply a marriage problem. Most victims I have known have framed the problem the same way at one point or another because of the exceedingly confusing nature of coercive control. As earlier chapters in this book have clearly demonstrated, domestic abuse is not a relationship issue that occurs "between" two people. Instead, it is one person exerting oppressive power and control over the other. When we mutualize the problem and minimize the dangers of abuse, the risks are substantial. Dynamics like this can make it very challenging for inexperienced and untrained helpers to know how to respond well.

Over the years, I have heard innumerable stories from victims about how well-meaning helpers actually made things worse. Whether they sought help from judges, court officials, law enforcement personnel, counselors, pastors, or even friends and family, they were unable to find the support they needed to move forward and thrive. Hosea 4:6 tells us that people perish for a lack of knowledge, and when it comes to advocating for victims of domestic abuse, a lack of knowledge can result in complete devastation or even death. Involving a well-trained and experienced advocate is a vital part of a wise response to this complex and difficult issue.

Trained advocates can help counselors, pastors, people helpers, and the victim to clear the confusion that so often exists when it comes to coercive control in relationships. They can meet with the victim, evaluate the situation, and give the care team an expert and concise assessment of what is happening. Their job is to assess any potential dangers to the woman and her children and make a safety plan if necessary. This is one of the most important reasons that counselors and pastors should include an advocate on their team. Their knowledge and experience provide an extra measure of protection for both the victim and those trying to help her. Although we have a nationwide network of volunteer advocates at Called to Peace Ministries, we still refer our counselees to advocates at local domestic violence agencies to make sure they have every possible resource available. This also reduces any potential liability to advocates in case the abuse escalates to homicide. In my years of experience with domestic abuse, I have found that homicides often occur in cases where there has never been any physical injury to the victim in the past. We can never be too cautious in these cases or predict when a case of abuse will escalate to the point of lethality.

Besides helping with safety planning, advocates can also identify how the abuse has impacted the survivor and her children. Some of the most common impacts are stress-related physical ailments, financial devastation, lack of stable housing and transportation, shared custody with an abusive parent, and constant fear about the abuser's potential actions. Once these impacts are identified, the advocate can then connect her to the appropriate resources and information to help her move forward. Advocates can lessen the load of counselors working with these victims, who are often women requiring more help than the average counselee. Since advocates usually have knowledge of local resources specific to victim needs, their assistance can save counselors a lot of time and effort.

In all they do, the best advocates never direct their counselees. That is the last thing women who have been oppressed need, even though they may want someone to tell them what to do. Directing victims of abuse simply prevents them from exercising their God-given agency. The Bible clearly testifies that God gives people choices, even if their choices might lead to negative consequences. One of the best examples of this is when he leads the children of Israel into the Promised Land and says, "I have set before you life and death, blessings and curses. Now choose life, so that you and your children may live . . ." (Deuteronomy 30:19b NIV). Isn't this what the best parents do? They teach their children to make wise decisions; they do not simply dictate their every move.

In the same way, wise advocates (and counselors) help victims of abuse look at their options so that they can decide how to move forward. They help restore agency to those who have not had freedom of choice for a very long time. Many women who have been oppressed in their homes are afraid to make decisions because they were ridiculed or punished if they took any initiative at home. It may take time for a victim of abuse to gather the strength to make decisions, and sometimes when she does, she may not make the best choices. I have seen this happen many times over the past few decades. However, I have also seen that those who connect with God and find healing eventually choose to consistently live for the glory of the One who set them free. Freedom does not come easily for one who has been oppressed and helpless, but an effective advocate can provide an extra measure of support to help them find a path forward. An advocate's presence in times of trouble can reflect God's heart to someone who has lost hope. Many times they offer extra support for issues that can be daunting for counselors, such as obtaining protective orders, understanding local custody laws, finding housing or financial assistance, and more.

Get Understanding (Proverbs 4:4b)

I am so grateful for God's heart for the helpless, and that he rescued me from an impossible situation. When I was trying to get away from the abuse I was suffering, I was astounded at the lack of understanding and resources I faced. When I reached out for help, I was disappointed time after time.[1] Whether it was law enforcement, the courts, my pastor, even friends and family, nobody knew how to help. Only God was able to make a way when there seemed to be no way. During that time of intense suffering, I promised God that if he let me live through it, I would one day help other women in the same situation. That promise has been easy to keep because once I escaped and told my story, I encountered scores of women facing the same obstacles. I became an advocate soon after getting out. Now, looking back on my years of advocacy work, I know that I have made many mistakes. A few times, I further endangered the women I was helping, as well as my children and myself, because of my lack of knowledge.

Understanding and knowledge are vital to good advocacy work. For this reason, you will notice that I primarily talk about trained

1. *Called to Peace: A Survivor's Guide to Finding Peace and Healing After Domestic Abuse* (Raleigh, NC: Blue Ink Press, 2018) recounts my entire story.

advocates in this chapter because I believe that the issues of domestic abuse and coercive control require expert help. In recent years, we have seen more counselors get training and expertise on domestic abuse, and some might take on some functions of the advocates' role out of necessity. That is why I often recommend that counselors dealing with domestic abuse take time to get training in advocacy. Because of the complex nature of abuse, it is helpful to have many sets of eyes on the situation.

Who Can Become an Advocate?

Anyone who has a heart to walk alongside those who are oppressed in their homes can do this work—both men and women. Counselors and pastors can also greatly benefit from advocacy training. There are several ways to get trained. Most state coalitions against domestic violence and local domestic violence programs have advocacy training to give the fundamentals. Usually these 40-hour trainings also involve a lot of compliance-related information for organizations receiving federal funds.

Called to Peace Ministries (CTPM), in conjunction with Dr. Debra Wingfield, has a one-year faith-based advocacy training (nearly 100 hours) that includes a practicum and mentoring. We have had people from all walks of life take the training—survivors, counselors, and pastors. Anyone who completes this one-year training can volunteer to work cases under the supervision of CTPM trainers and staff. It's an excellent opportunity to get supervised experience in advocacy. We ask survivors who want to become advocates to take time to pursue their own healing before taking cases so that they are not overly triggered and reactive when they begin the work. Most of the time, men who take these courses provide support to victims by providing education and resources. They can also help by providing education to pastors, counselors, and other helpers through our church partnership program.

Church leaders can reach out to CTPM to request help from a trained advocate or one of the two pastors on staff who serve as church liaisons. These pastors are trained advocates who head up our church partnership program, in which we provide training and ongoing consultation to churches working cases of domestic abuse. We recommend that our church partners designate at least two members of their congregations to sign up to receive training as advocates. Our goal is not just to help churches deal with this issue, but to equip them to better respond to this difficult issue.

Misconceptions about Advocacy

In any discussion of advocacy, I think it's a good idea to cover what advocates *don't* do. I have found that there are some common misunderstandings about what the position involves. At the same time, many untrained "advocates/activists" do act in ways that perpetuate these misconceptions. However, good advocates know better. Well-trained advocates are taught not to direct victims of coercive control, but to instead restore their agency. This means that they don't tell them what to believe, whether they should get a divorce, or whether they should leave or stay. They don't blame victims for the abuse they experienced by implying that they did something to cause it. Instead, they provide encouragement, help them explore their options, and do their best to help them stay safe. In addition, they don't try to rescue victims, but allow them to make their own decisions regarding the future.

The role of an advocate is unique. It does not involve counseling or therapy; rather, it deals with logistics and practicalities. It is usually far more time-consuming than counseling because the advocate helps the victim explore her options and negotiate multiple barriers in a variety of life realms. These barriers include ongoing court cases, financial challenges, housing and transportation needs, communication with a guardian ad litem, church leaders, child protective services, etc. This role can last for years because even after separation or divorce, abusers continue to create new challenges and barriers. It is not uncommon for court cases involving equitable distribution and custody to drag on for years as abusers often use the courts to continue their abuse. Through all of these challenges, the advocate represents the victim's best interests, always allowing her to take the lead on how it plays out.

Ways Advocates Help

While the primary role of advocates is to support survivors through the many challenges they face, the goal of advocacy is to help prevent further damage and attain the best possible outcome for survivors. Sadly, in cases of coercive control, the result is usually painful no matter what they choose to do. Basically, the best outcome is usually the one that is least harmful to everyone involved. Since domestic abuse is complex, and each case is so unique, advocates often need to be creative in helping their counselees find answers to the dilemmas they face. This means there is no way to fully describe how advocates function in a single chapter, but the list below contains the most common services they offer victims.

- Meet with the victim/survivor to help identify abusive patterns in their home.
- Give other helpers a concise assessment of what is happening and the impacts that the abuse has had on the victim and her children.
- Assess possible dangers/lethality risk and create a safety plan to protect her and her children (see appendix B).
- Help document (and find a safe place to store) evidence of the abuse to help discern whether there is sufficient proof to obtain a protective order and to help with custody issues.
- Help her prepare for and accompany her to court. (Court situations are usually highly intimidating to survivors, and knowledge of how family courts tend to deal with domestic abuse is important.)
- Research local resources and make referrals to domestic abuse/trauma-informed professionals (counselors, attorneys, support

groups, etc.) and agencies that help with practical needs (housing, transportation, financial assistance, resources for kids, etc.).

- Meet with team members on her behalf to make sure her concerns are being addressed, and to give the survivor's perspective on the abuser's progress or lack thereof.
- Be available to support her in meetings with counselors, pastors, court officials, child protective services, etc.
- Help prepare victim impact statements.
- Provide education on domestic abuse and tools to equip her and those seeking to help.
- Help her think through all possible scenarios, understanding that there is no easy solution. (If she stays it will be hard, and if she leaves it will be hard.)
- Regularly assess the situation to identify new threats and update the safety plan as needed.
- Provide spiritual encouragement. While this is not generally considered a function of advocacy, the very presence of a Christian advocate can remind counselees of God's love and care for them and help them know they are valued.

An advocate's work is indispensable in cases of domestic abuse. Just like our Advocate on High, they come alongside those who feel helpless to provide practical help in a time of need. I can think of no better way to show just how vital advocates are than to close with these quotes from survivors:

> I was in a desolate place in my life because of the domestic abuse I suffered until I finally got an advocate. For the first time in a very long time, I felt understood. The connection I experienced with her changed my life—it restored my hope and helped me believe that God was for me.—LP

> After years of abuse that left me feeling alone, worthless, and confused, my CTPM advocate helped me navigate the many

challenges I faced. She was the literal hands and feet of Jesus to me.—CG

When I read quotes like these, I can't help but smile and think that God must be smiling too. He loves it when his children follow in his footsteps. The concept of advocacy originated with him, and I know he is pleased when his children answer his call to seek justice and defend the oppressed (Isaiah 1:17 NIV). This is the heart of our heavenly advocate.

APPENDIX A

• • • •

Basic Abuse Screening Questions[1]

Darby A. Strickland

Whether you suspect abuse or it is disclosed to you, you will need to determine its scope and severity. Remember oppression is fueled by a pernicious sense of entitlement. Oppressors use a variety of punishments to make their world the way they want it. Abuse is not always immediately evident. While some punishing behaviors will easily be labeled as abusive—such as choking, raping, and punching—other punishments might take more investigation to determine whether they are used to gain coercive control—like driving erratically, unwanted peeking while showering, or verbal tirades.

Often we have to wrestle with the question of when does the punishment or punishments become so severe they are called *abuse*? When it is not immediately clear, you will have to consider a variety of factors. Seek to determine whether there are patterns of punishing behaviors and what each behavior affords its perpetrator. You will want to use the screening questions below to uncover punishing behaviors. As you do, be alert to the following patterns:

1. In her book, *Is It Abuse?* (Phillipsburg, NJ: P&R Publications, 2020), Darby devotes time to providing you with careful assessment questions for each type of abuse so that you can make careful and accurate assessments as to whether a situation rises to the level of oppression.

Does the behavior establish coercive control of the victim?

Does it seek to change a victim's current or future behavior?

Does it leave the victim feeling fearful or anxious?

Please keep in mind that answering yes to any one of the screening questions does not necessarily mean that the relationship is abusive. If you get an affirmative answer to a question, ask for an example. After a potential victim shares one story with you, ask her if this has happened before and, if so, would she be willing to share the most extreme example she can recall.

It might take time to gather the needed information to discern whether abuse is present. And it usually takes time for a victim to trust you enough to disclose key information. If you are unsure if the sin patterns you are uncovering rise to the level of abuse, take the needed time to gather more information while being mindful of potential safety issues.

Basic Abuse Screening Questions:

- Have you ever been threatened or physically hurt in this relationship?
- Have you ever been an unwilling participant in a sexual act?
- Do you ever feel fearful around your spouse?
- Do you have the freedom to be yourself, make decisions, give input, and say no to things?
- Have you ever been touched by your spouse in a way that made you uncomfortable?
- How can you tell when your spouse is angry? Be specific. What does it look like? What is said? Done?
- When discussing hard things, what are some ways that disagreement is expressed? (Mocking, walking away, rolling eyes, hovering, or throwing things?)
- What happens when you try to share a differing opinion?
- Does your spouse ever ignore you? If so, for how long and when?
- What happens if you let him/her down?

- Do you feel pressure to do things you do not want to do? Sexually?
- Does your spouse remind you of times that you sinned against them? When and how?
- Remember, you will want to talk to the victim without her oppressor present and face-to-face, as her communications might be monitored.

APPENDIX B

....

Sample Safety Plan

A safety plan is a way to help you identify possible things you can do to protect yourself (and your children) when your partner becomes violent toward you.[1] This plan may make you aware of your personal resources as well as those in your community. It can also help you in identifying the signs and situations that happen before your partner chooses to become abusive. Most importantly, a safety plan helps you discover steps you can take for protection against your partner's threats of abuse and injury. Remember, you are the expert when it comes to knowing what abusive situations may occur in your relationship with your partner. Studies show that the abuse you have experienced usually repeats itself and often gets worse. It is important that you have a plan to help you be safe if your partner chooses to threaten or hurt you again.

Answering the following questions will help create your own safety plan:

1. Adapted from unknown source by Diana Philip, Denton County Friends of the Family, Inc., Texas, 1995.

1. What are some of the kinds of cues, behaviors, or circumstances that are present before abusive situations happen? (i.e., time of day, substance abuse, discussion about money, locations, certain relatives or friends visiting, stress level of partner, etc.)

2. What kinds of things have you tried to protect yourself (and your children) in the past? Which of these things have worked and which would you use again?

3. What situations are you most afraid of?

4. What kinds of things have you thought of that may help you with the things you fear most?

5. What things can you do to increase your independence? (open credit or bank accounts in your name, take classes to improve job skills, etc.)

6. What kinds of legal resources in your community are available to you? (Look up phone numbers and list where to apply for a

protective order, file for divorce, establish custody and visitation orders, etc.)

7. What types of medical services in your community are available to you?

8. What types of arrangements can you make to improve your safety at work or school? (Change your routes, screen your calls, change arrival and departure times, consider safety while traveling, etc.)

9. What can you do to improve your safety at home? (Change locks, buy safety devices such as security cameras, inform neighbors and landlord to call the police if they hear a disturbance, purchase a cell phone, etc.)

10. What types of things can you do to improve the safety and protection of your children or other family members in your home? (Inform school/day care of situation, practice safety plan with the family, etc.)

If your partner becomes threatening or abusive, you may choose to leave your home, even if only temporarily. You can do the following things to prepare for such a situation:

1. Think of where to leave extra money, keys, copies of important documents, and clothes at a safe place that is easy to get to:

2. Practice how to get out of your home safely. The following plan would be best for you (your children, family members and pets) if you need to leave quickly:

3. You can call 911 for the police to come and intervene. You can make up a code word to use with your children, family, friends, and neighbors when you need the police. The code word you would use and the people you can ask for help are:

4. Relatives or friends you can call for support and/or a safe place to stay:

5. The phone number for the local domestic violence program/shelter where you can stay in safety and receive support in deciding what to do next is:

6. Other things you can do:

7. The following items may be important to take with you when leaving your home:

Identification	Insurance papers	Social security cards
Driver's license	House & car keys	Welfare identification
Birth certificate	Medications	School records
Money/credit cards	Small salable objects	Apartment lease/house deed
Bank/checkbooks	Address books	Photos & negatives
Green card/work permit	Passports	Vehicle titles
Diaries & journals	Income tax returns	Medical records
Protective Order	Divorce papers	Custody/visitation orders

APPENDIX C

....

Sample Release of Information (ROI)

Both victims and perpetrators of abuse are, first and foremost, image-bearers of God. The image of God has been corrupted in them, as in all of us, in body and soul, by the brokenness that arises from living in a broken world, the sins of others against them, and their own personal sin against a holy God and against other image-bearers. Some of the descriptions of that brokenness may constitute individually identifiable personal information that may relate to an image-bearer's mental or physical health. Any "individually identifiable health information" about a person's mental or physical health, including certain aspects of his spiritual health that also may correlate with his mental or physical health belongs to the individual and should be handled with careful discretion, whether or not it is deemed to be "protected health information" (PHI) under the Health Insurance Portability and Accountability Act of 1996 (HIPAA). A counselee provides informed consent at the outset of a counseling relationship that they understand how counseling will work, including how confidentiality works and how their individually identifiable personal information will be used.

Domestic abuse care, in particular, is more effective when there can be some degree of collaboration and coordination between members of the counselee's shepherding team. Counselors, church staff, and care team members honor the confidential information of their members/counselees by getting the counselee's written consent to share information within a limited scope via a signed Release of Information (ROI).

In my (Greg Wilson's) counseling practice, I use the following language in my standard release of information:

I hereby direct, authorize, and release my counselor at Soul Care Associates (Counselor's Name) to release my personal health information, including my status as a counselee or former counselee of the counselor, the dates and times of service, billing/invoicing requests, and information discussed in session, as well as anything else specified below:

- Medical history and evaluations
- Mental health evaluations
- Developmental and/or social history
- Educational records
- Progress notes and treatment or closing summary
- Other: ____________________

To: (Name and contact information of person to whom information may be released)

For the following purpose: (Short description of the purpose for which information may be released)

This consent will expire on the following date: (Date that consent will expire)

By signing this authorization form: I understand that my records contain information regarding my mental health. I give specific permission for this information to be released. I understand that my records are protected under state and federal law and cannot be disclosed without my written consent unless otherwise provided for by law. I understand that this authorization is voluntary, and I may revoke this consent at any time by providing written notice, and after (states vary, usually one year) this consent automatically expires. I have been informed what information will be given, its purpose, and who will receive the information. I understand that I have a right to receive a copy of this authorization. I understand that I have a right to refuse to sign this authorization.

Counselee's Signature and Date

While the wording above is all pretty standard, I do recommend that readers review other release of information forms, as well as having an attorney review all of the forms that they use with counselees.

Other sample release of information forms can be found in the following Christian counseling resources:

> Randolph K. Sanders, ed., "Appendix 2: Sample Forms," in *Christian Counseling Ethics: A Handbook for Psychologists, Therapists, and Pastors*, Second Ed. (Downer's Grove, IL: IVP Academic, 2013), 531.
>
> John C. Thomas and Lisa Sosin, "Appendix G: Release of Information Form," in *Therapeutic Expedition: Equipping the Christian Counselor for the Journey* (Nashville: B&H Publishing Group, 2011), 599.

. . . .

Glossary of Terms

Advocate (noun)—a helper committed to walking with a victim, by providing resources, creating a safety plan, helping her through the court process, acting as a liaison with other care team members, and encouraging her spiritually.

Agency—the ability to assert one's will and make decisions.

Batterer Intervention and Prevention Programs (BIPP)—a series of classes that focus on changing the dynamics of domestic violence. A secular program often supported by the state and mandated by courts, but useful to others as well.

Care plan—a specific plan for an abuse victim that includes her ensuring own safety (and that of her children), confronting her husband, and counseling for all members of the family.

Care team—a team of people in the local church that work together to help families ensnared by abuse. This includes pastors, counselors, advocates, mentors, and others central to the care and confrontation needed in cases of domestic abuse.

Community Coordinated Response (CCR)—a collaboration of community agencies to help those affected by domestic violence. This may include advocates, prosecutors, law enforcement, and others.

Domestic Abuse/Domestic Violence—a pattern of coercive control toward an intimate partner or children in the home. This pattern of cruelty appears in any means of relating—physical, sexual, economic, mental, verbal, or spiritual.

Domestic Abuser/Perpetrator/Batterer/Oppressor—one who has used abuse toward a relationship partner in the household in order to gain control.

Domestic Abuse Victim/Survivor—one who has endured abuse from a relationship partner in the household.

Dominion—having control over an area of life and being able to make decisions in that area.

Intimate Partner Violence (IPV)—violence toward a spouse or partner, which has historically referred to a man mistreating a woman.

Men of Peace (MOP)—biblically based education and accountability group for men in the church who have been perpetrators of abuse.

Release of Information form (ROI)—signed documents that grant permission of a counselee to share with others on a care team any individually identifiable health information about their mental or physical health, including certain aspects of their spiritual health that may correlate with mental or physical health.

Safety assessment—a series of specific questions asked of the victim in order to determine the current safety level of the victim and her children.

Safety plan—a detailed plan created by the oppressed and her counselor to maintain safety in the event of a dangerous abuse situation.

Trauma—an event that deeply harmed an individual and left lasting adverse effects on the individual's mental, physical, and emotional health.

....

Recommended Resources

Articles and Blogs

- Lundy Bancroft, "Guide for Men Who Are Serious about Changing, Part 1," personal blog, accessed April 24, 2023, https://lundybancroft.com/articles/guide-for-men-changing-part-1/.
    - ———. "Guide for Men Who Are Serious about Changing, Part 2," personal blog, accessed April 24, 2023, https://lundybancroft.com/articles/guide-for-men-changing-part-2/.
- Chelsey Gordon, "Disappointment Upon Disappointment," personal blog, July 27, 2020, https://cgordon183.wixsite.com/perceiveandconsider/post/disappointment-upon-disappointment.
    - ———. "Domestic Abuse Victims: Sinners or Sufferers?" The Institute for Biblical Counseling and Discipleship (IBCD), October 8, 2020, https://ibcd.org/domestic-abuse-victims-sinners-or-sufferers/.
    - ———. "How Can God Use My Survivor Story? (Part One)," July 27, 2020, personal blog, https://cgordon183.wixsite.com/perceiveandconsider/post/how-can-god-use-my-survivor-story-part-one.
    - ———. "Not As They Seem: Anticipating Deception in Domestic Abuse Cases," The Institute for Biblical Counseling and Discipleship (IBCD), October 15, 2020, https://ibcd.org/

not-as-they-seem-anticipating-deception-in-domestic-abuse-cases/.

- ———. "Why the Gospel Is Especially Good News for Domestic Abuse Victims," The Institute for Biblical Counseling and Discipleship (IBCD), October 22, 2020, https://ibcd.org/why-the-gospel-is-especially-good-news-for-domestic-abuse-victims-2/.
- ———. "Personal Soul Care for Those in Domestic Abuse Counseling," The Institute for Biblical Counseling and Discipleship (IBCD), February 25, 2021, https://ibcd.org/personal-soul-care-for-those-in-domestic-abuse-counseling/.

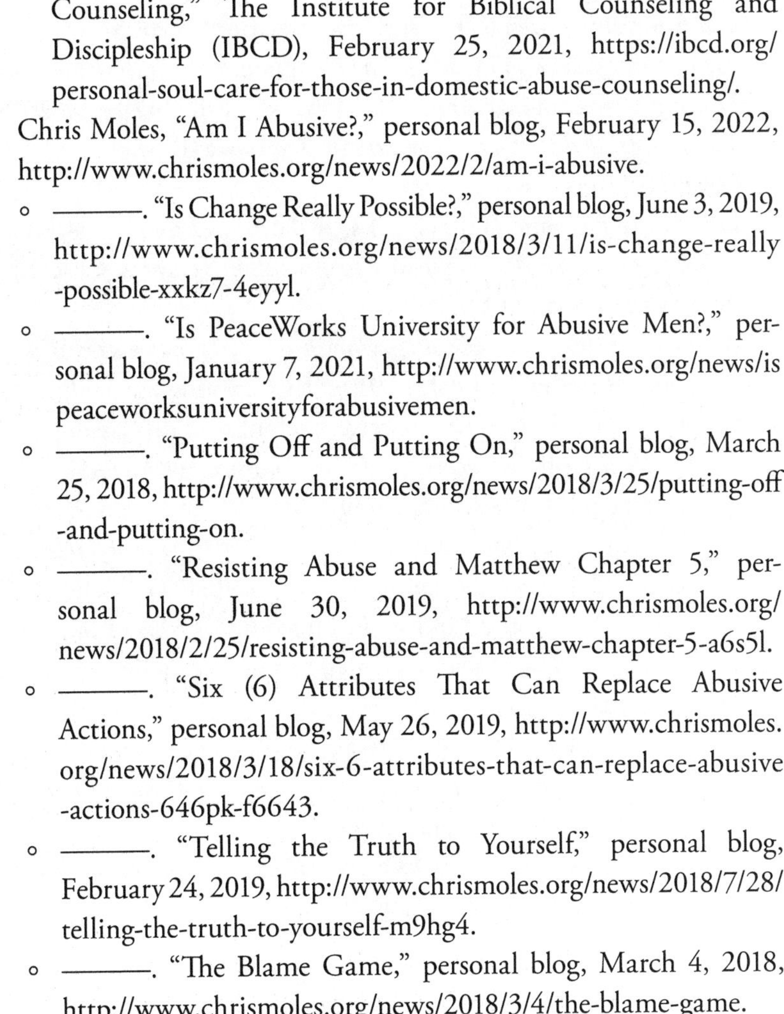

- Chris Moles, "Am I Abusive?," personal blog, February 15, 2022, http://www.chrismoles.org/news/2022/2/am-i-abusive.
  - ———. "Is Change Really Possible?," personal blog, June 3, 2019, http://www.chrismoles.org/news/2018/3/11/is-change-really-possible-xxkz7-4eyyl.
  - ———. "Is PeaceWorks University for Abusive Men?," personal blog, January 7, 2021, http://www.chrismoles.org/news/is peaceworksuniversityforabusivemen.
  - ———. "Putting Off and Putting On," personal blog, March 25, 2018, http://www.chrismoles.org/news/2018/3/25/putting-off-and-putting-on.
  - ———. "Resisting Abuse and Matthew Chapter 5," personal blog, June 30, 2019, http://www.chrismoles.org/news/2018/2/25/resisting-abuse-and-matthew-chapter-5-a6s5l.
  - ———. "Six (6) Attributes That Can Replace Abusive Actions," personal blog, May 26, 2019, http://www.chrismoles.org/news/2018/3/18/six-6-attributes-that-can-replace-abusive-actions-646pk-f6643.
  - ———. "Telling the Truth to Yourself," personal blog, February 24, 2019, http://www.chrismoles.org/news/2018/7/28/telling-the-truth-to-yourself-m9hg4.
  - ———. "The Blame Game," personal blog, March 4, 2018, http://www.chrismoles.org/news/2018/3/4/the-blame-game.

- Jonathon Woodyard, "We Are Complementarians, but We Do Not Believe a Wife Should Submit to an Abusive Husband," *Theology Along the Way*, May 7, 2018, https://theologyalongtheway.org/2018/05/07/we-do-not-believe-a-wife-should-submit-to-an-abusive-husband-a-joint-statement/.

Books

- Lundy Bancroft, *Why Does He Do That? Inside the Minds of Angry and Controlling Men* (New York: Berkley Books, 2003).
- Joy Forrest, *Called to Peace: A Survivor's Guide to Finding Peace and Healing after Domestic Abuse* (Raleigh, NC: Blue Ink Press, 2018).
- ———. *Called to Peace: Companion Workbook* (Raleigh, NC: Blue Ink Press, 2019).
- Julie Ganschow and Bill Schlacks, *A Biblical Counselor's Approach to Marital Abuse: Roadmap to Reunification* (Kansas City, MO: Pure Water Press, 2018).
- Brad Hambrick, gen. ed., *Becoming a Church That Cares Well for the Abused* (Nashville: B&H, 2019). This training curriculum can be found in book form or as twelve free online video lessons.
- ———. *Self-Centered Spouse: Help for Chronically Broken Marriages* (Phillipsburg, NJ: P&R Publishing, 2014).
- Judith Herman, *Trauma and Recovery: The Aftermath of Violence—from Domestic Abuse to Political Terror* (New York: Basic Books, 1997).
- Justin S. Holcomb and Lindsey A. Holcomb, *Is It My Fault? Hope and Healing for Those Suffering Domestic Violence* (Chicago: Moody Publishers, 2014).
- Edward S. Kubany, Mari A. McCaig, and Janet Laconsay, *Healing the Trauma of Domestic Violence: A Workbook for Women* (Oakland, New Harbinger Publications, 2004).
- Diane Langberg, *Suffering and the Heart of God: How Trauma Destroys and Christ Restores* (Greensboro, NC: New Growth Press, 2015).

- Herbert Vander Lugt, *God's Protection of Women: When Abuse Is Worse Than Divorce* (Our Daily Bread Ministries). Free e-book: https://discoveryseries.org/courses/gods-protection-of-women/.
- Chris Moles, *The Heart of Domestic Abuse: Gospel Solutions for Men Who Use Control and Violence in the Home* (Bemidji, MN: Focus Publishing, 2015).
- Welby O'Brien, *Formerly a Wife: A Survival Guide for Women Facing the Pain and Disruption of Divorce* (Sisters, OR: Trusted Books, 2018).
- Jeremy Pierre and Greg Wilson, *When Home Hurts: A Guide for Responding Wisely to Domestic Abuse in Your Church* (Ross-shire, Scotland: Christian Focus Publishing, 2021).
- Stuart Scott, *From Pride to Humility: A Biblical Perspective* (Bemidji, MN: Focus Publishing, 2002).
- Darby A. Strickland, *Domestic Abuse: Recognize, Respond, Rescue* (minibook) (Phillipsburg, NJ: P&R Publishing, 2018).
- ———. *Is It Abuse? A Biblical Guide to Identifying Domestic Abuse and Helping Victims* (Phillipsburg, NJ: P&R Publishing, 2020).
- ———. *Something Scary Happened: Helping Children through Trauma* (children's illustrated book) (Greensboro, NC: New Growth Press, 2023).
- ———. *When Children Experience Trauma: What to Do When Something Scary Happens* (minibook) (Greensboro, NC: New Growth Press, 2023).
- Helen Thorne, *Walking with Domestic Abuse Sufferers* (London: SPCK, 2018).
- Steven R. Tracy and Celestia G. Tracy, *Mending the Soul: Understanding and Healing Abuse* (Grand Rapids: Zondervan Reflective, 2022).
- Leslie Vernick, *The Emotionally Destructive Marriage: How to Find Your Voice and Reclaim Your Hope* (Colorado Springs: WaterBrook Press, 2013).

- ———. *The Emotionally Destructive Relationship: Seeing It, Stopping It, Surviving It* (Eugene, OR: Harvest House Publishers, 2007).
- Edward T. Welch, *Shame Interrupted: How God Lifts the Pain of Worthlessness and Rejection* (Greensboro, NC: New Growth Press, 2012).

Training Resources

- Counseling Care for Domestic Abuse, 9-video case series from The Institute for Biblical Counseling and Discipleship (IBCD), DVD, https://ibcd.org/product/counseling-care-for-domestic-abuse/.
- Brad Hambrick, gen. ed., *Becoming a Church That Cares Well for the Abused*, free online video training curriculum, https://churchcares.com/.
- Chris Moles, The Heart of Domestic Abuse: Step by Step Abuser Intervention for Biblical Counselors, online course, https://chrismoles.podia.com/the-heart-of-domestic-abuse-online-course.
- PeaceWorks University, an online membership site that exists to train and support helpers in a variety of ministry contexts to address domestic violence with the gospel of peace. http://www.chrismoles.org/coaching-with-chris.
- Darby Strickland and Edward T. Welch, "Trauma: Bearing the Unbearable," digital download, 2019 CCEF Regional Conference, https://www.ccef.org/shop/product/trauma-bearing-the-unbearable-digital-download/.

Organizations and Additional Resources

- Called to Peace Ministries, www.calledtopeace.org
- ChrisMoles.org
- DarbyStrickland.com
- The Domestic Abuse Hotline: 1-800-799-7233. Domestic Violence Support, National Domestic Violence Hotline (thehotline.org)

- Focus Ministries, https://www.focusministries1.org
- *The PeaceWorks Podcast.* A weekly podcast featuring teaching from Chris Moles, interviews with experts, and stories from survivors. http://www.chrismoles.org/podcast.

• • • •

Contributor Bios

Beth Broom, LPC-S, CCTP-II, owns a private counseling practice specializing in trauma healing. She also serves as a deacon of care at The Village Church Denton in Denton, Texas. Beth is the founder and director of Christian Trauma Healing Network, a nonprofit organization designed to bring trauma care and healing to Christians in the church and society. She cohosts the podcast *Counsel for Life*, engaging conversations about mental health and the Christian life. She is married to Kenny, and they have three children—Sarah, Levi, and Elijah.

Kïrsten Christianson is a CCEF-trained biblical counselor who serves through her ministry, Side-by-Side Biblical Counseling. She also consults with churches across the United States on congregational care. She loves helping elders care well for their flocks as they face all kinds of crises and complex situations, including abuse. She loves sharpening gospel conversations, Caribou's dark hot chocolate, books, word games, and Alabama football!

Joy Forrest, MABC, is a counselor, author, and advocate who has worked in domestic violence advocacy since 1997. She is the executive director of Called to Peace Ministries and is the author of *Called to Peace: A Survivor's Guide to Finding Peace & Healing After Domestic*

Abuse and the *Called to Peace Companion Workbook*. Joy is a contributing expert for DivorceCare's divorce recovery curriculum and the IBCD's Counseling Care for Domestic Abuse videos.

Chris Moles, MA, is senior pastor of the Chapel in Winfield, West Virginia, and an ordained minister with the Christian and Missionary Alliance. He is a certified biblical counselor with the Association of Certified Biblical Counselors and the International Association of Biblical Counselors. Moles is a contributor to the West Virginia intervention curriculum used throughout the state prisons, correctional facilities, and community organizations. He is the author of *The Heart of Domestic Abuse* and a contributor to *Becoming a Church that Cares Well for the Abused.*

Darby A. Strickland, MDiv, is a faculty member and counselor at the Christian Counseling & Educational Foundation (CCEF). She is a contributor to *Becoming a Church that Cares Well for the Abused* and author of *Is It Abuse? A Biblical Guide to Identifying Domestic Abuse and Helping Victims*. She writes regularly for the *Journal of Biblical Counseling*. Darby and her husband, John, have three children.

Greg Wilson, DEdMin, LPC Supervisor, is a licensed professional counselor and leads Soul Care Associates, a counseling and consulting practice in Texas. He specializes in counseling victims and perpetrators of domestic abuse, as well as counseling adolescents, men, couples, and families through issues such as depression, anxiety, abuse, addictions, trauma, and relational conflict. He also consults with leaders of churches and other organizations on adopting best practices for care. He is the coauthor (with Jeremy Pierre) of *When Home Hurts: A Guide for Responding Wisely to Domestic Abuse in Your Church.*